Quick Clojure

Effective Functional Programming

Mark McDonnell

Apress®

Quick Clojure: Effective Functional Programming

Mark McDonnell
Southend-on-Sea, UK

ISBN-13 (pbk): 978-1-4842-2951-4   ISBN-13 (electronic): 978-1-4842-2952-1
DOI 10.1007/978-1-4842-2952-1

Library of Congress Control Number: 2017952537

Cover image by Freepik (`www.freepik.com`)

Managing Director: Welmoed Spahr
Editorial Director: Todd Green
Acquisitions Editor: Steve Anglin
Development Editor: Matthew Moodie
Technical Reviewer: Massimo Nardone
Coordinating Editor: Mark Powers
Copy Editor: April Rondeau

Distributed to the book trade worldwide by Springer Science+Business Media New York, 233 Spring Street, 6th Floor, New York, NY 10013. Phone 1-800-SPRINGER, fax (201) 348-4505, e-mail `orders-ny@springer-sbm.com`, or visit `www.springeronline.com`. Apress Media, LLC is a California LLC, and the sole member (owner) is Springer Science + Business Media Finance Inc (SSBM Finance Inc). SSBM Finance Inc is a **Delaware** corporation.

For information on translations, please e-mail `rights@apress.com`, or visit `http://www.apress.com/rights-permissions`.

Apress titles may be purchased in bulk for academic, corporate, or promotional use. eBook versions and licenses are also available for most titles. For more information, reference our Print and eBook Bulk Sales web page at `http://www.apress.com/bulk-sales`.

Any source code or other supplementary material referenced by the author in this book is available to readers on GitHub via the book's product page, located at `www.apress.com/9781484229514`. For more detailed information, please visit `http://www.apress.com/source-code`.

Printed on acid-free paper

This is dedicated to my wife Catherine and also to my mum and dad.

*They have a limitless belief in my ability to succeed,
and without them I would certainly have failed.*

Contents at a Glance

Contents

About the Author

Mark McDonnell works for BuzzFeed as a senior software engineer. Previously, he was a principal engineer with the BBC and also with Storm Creative. He is a polyglot programmer with experience in Clojure, Go, Python, and many other languages. He has published books with Apress as well as self-published. He loves playing jazz guitar, watching mixed-martial arts, and enjoying life with his wife, Catherine, and their two cats.

About the Technical Reviewer

 **Massimo Nardone** has more than 23 years of experience in security, web/mobile development, cloud, and IT architecture. His true IT passions are security and Android.

He has been programming and teaching how to program with Android, Perl, PHP, Java, VB, Python, C/C++, and MySQL for more than 20 years.

He holds a Master of Science degree in Computing Science from the University of Salerno, Italy.

He has worked as a project manager, software engineer, research engineer, chief security architect, information security manager, PCI/SCADA auditor, and senior lead IT security/cloud/SCADA architect for many years.

Technical skills include security, Android, cloud, Java, MySQL, Drupal, Cobol, Perl, web and mobile development, MongoDB, D3, Joomla, Couchbase, C/C++, WebGL, Python, Pro Rails, Django CMS, Jekyll, Scratch, and more.

He worked as visiting lecturer and supervisor for exercises at the Networking Laboratory of the Helsinki University of Technology (Aalto University). He holds four international patents (PKI, SIP, SAML, and Proxy areas).

He currently works as chief information security officer (CISO) for Cargotec Oyj, and he is a member of the board for ISACA's Finland chapter.

Massimo has reviewed more than 40 IT books for different publishers, and he is the coauthor of *Pro Android Games* (Apress, 2015).

Acknowledgments

As you get older, you typically find the adage "less is more" to be the appropriate way to go for most things. With this in mind, I'd like to acknowledge the reviewers of this book, who helped round off some of the rough edges into something altogether more cohesive.

I'd also like to acknowledge the patience of my wife (Catherine), who recognized early on that there was only one thing better than having a book published with your name on it . . . and that's having two published books.

Introduction

This is a book about the Clojure programming language. Chances are you're already somewhat familiar with the language and you're keen to expose yourself to more of it. Maybe you're learning Clojure for fun, or maybe it's because you're starting a new job that requires you to work with it more. Either way, I'm sure you'll learn some useful things about the language and will enjoy programming in it for many years to come.

We're going to start off fairly slow and pick up speed as we go through the chapters. There is no thread that ties all the chapters together. Once you have the basic syntax understood, you should be able to drop into any chapter safely.

You may find some chapters are shorter than others; this is simply because I wanted conciseness wherever possible. We could try and cover every conceivable feature in the Clojure language (for which there is a lot of ground to cover), but let's face it—this would become one of those books you never finish. It would sit on a shelf or become a door stop because it's too big to feasibly read through.

I wanted this book to be as short as possible, to give you the information you need and then allow you the freedom to investigate beyond your own understanding when the time comes for you to need to know something that might not have been covered within these pages.

I wish you all the best with your journey into Clojure. I'm sure you're itching to get started. So, let's do that . . .

CHAPTER 1

What Is Clojure?

Clojure[1] is a functional, symbiotic, and homoiconic programming language.

OK, for an opening line I'm sure you will agree that's a bit of a mouthful. So, let's break that sentence down a bit and focus on the words *functional, symbiotic,* and *homoiconic* in order to understand what they mean.

Fear not if the following descriptions end up sounding like academic nonsense; we'll be covering these concepts in more detail as we make our way through the various chapters of this book, and you'll come to realize that they do, in fact, have very practical usage in Clojure.

- **Functional**: where functions are first-class citizens and mutating state is frowned upon

- **Symbiotic**: the language is intended to be run atop a host environment

- **Homoiconic**: "code is data" — this helps facilitate a macro system for rewriting the language

---

Note Clojure also supports optional typing,[2] although that feature is outside the scope of this book.

Typically, when reading about Clojure you will see these terms (functional, symbiotic, homoiconic) mentioned quite a lot, and so it can be useful to become better acquainted with them and with what people mean when they use these terms in the context of the Clojure language.

The main platform Clojure supports is JVM[3] (Java Virtual Machine). But Clojure also supports any platform that can execute the JavaScript engine, such as a web browser, by way of an offshoot of the language called ClojureScript.[4] ClojureScript is a compiler that transforms Clojure code into JavaScript code.

---

[1]http://clojure.org/
[2]https://github.com/clojure/core.typed
[3]http://en.wikipedia.org/wiki/Java_virtual_machine
[4]https://github.com/clojure/clojurescript

© Mark McDonnell 2017
M. McDonnell, *Quick Clojure*, DOI 10.1007/978-1-4842-2952-1_1

Clojure also works with the Common Language Runtime (CLR), which is the execution engine of Microsoft's .NET Framework.

■ **Note**　In this book, we focus exclusively on the JVM implementation of the Clojure programming language.

Clojure is a Lisp.[5] Lisp is a programming language originally designed in 1958. It has a very distinct syntax that makes it stand out from other modern programming languages. Languages such as Clojure build upon Lisp's structural basis (we'll learn more about this in the next chapter). The Lisp syntax is elegant and concise, and consequently affords us the ability to be very expressive. If you're unfamiliar with what the Lisp syntax looks like, don't worry, as we'll see examples of this as we go along.

If you're impatient, then the following snippet in Listing 1-1 is a small piece of code to at least give you an idea of what Clojure looks like (although at this point in time it obviously won't make much sense if you're new to Lisp and/or Clojure):

Listing 1-1. Demonstration of Clojure/Lisp Syntax

```
(def base-credentials {:client-config {:protocol "http"}})

(defn cred [{:keys [:Host :HostPort]}]
  (assoc base-credentials :endpoint (str Host ":" HostPort)))

(cred {:Host "localhost" :HostPort 8080})
```

There are many interesting aspects that make up the Clojure programming ecosystem, and although most of the really important items will be covered, it's worth noting that I'm not aiming to include every possible feature or detail, because then the focus of the book would become diluted and not be as palatable for beginners.

Clojure has a lot of complex moving parts, and so the idea is to help readers get up and running with Clojure and be able to play around with some of the language's most interesting features without getting bogged down with too many implementation details.

Why Should You Care?

Clojure is fun. No, really!

But, more practically, it makes developing solutions to complex problems trivial, thanks to the language's support for immutability, its multitude of concurrency mechanisms, and a very strong core library of functions (again, don't worry if those words mean nothing to you, as we'll cover all of these details in subsequent chapters).

You can even change the Clojure programming language itself to suit your requirements via a mechanism known as Macros. Macros is such an incredibly powerful feature that I really wish it were available in other programming languages I use. If you want to add a new type of flow control that the language doesn't natively support, then no problem; you can write it yourself dynamically with Clojure code! We'll see this in action later on.

---

[5]http://en.wikipedia.org/wiki/Lisp_%28programming_language%29

One of the oft-cited facts about Clojure is that the creator, Rich Hickey, spent *two years* on the design of the language before starting the arduous task of actually building and implementing Clojure.

This may sound like a pointless "fun fact," but after you begin writing Clojure code you'll soon start to understand why developers like to refer back to how long it took to design the language. It has meant Clojure was able to retrospectively pick all the good bits from other programming languages while also filtering out previous bad decisions, leaving you with a new programming language that ends up resolving a lot of otherwise contentious design issues.

The Name?

The word *Clojure* and where it comes from is a typical discussion point for Clojurists. Although, I'm not sure why, considering Rich Hickey (author of Clojure) has long since confirmed that the name is a combination of the following:

- C#

- Lisp

- Java

(C)(L)o(J)ure
Clojure is pronounced (in the author's own words):

> *exactly like closure, where the s/j has the zh sound as in azure, pleasure etc*

—Rich Hickey (Google Groups Discussion[6])

Getting Started

The first thing we're going to need is a REPL (REPL is an acronym for "Read Eval Print Loop"). Effectively, a REPL is a way for you to execute arbitrary pieces of code and to see the results, a form of "interactive development." You'll find as we go along that Clojure's workflow is very tightly integrated with the concept of using a REPL, and so that's why we'll be starting there.

You'll find most other languages also have REPLs:

- Node

- Ruby

- PHP

- Python

---

[6]Google Groups Discussion https://goo.gl/zs7Ux0

■ **Note**   Most of our time in this book will be spent using a REPL. It can be slow to start up initially, but we only have to do it once.

Leiningen—which to this day I forget how to pronounce properly—is a complete project automation and build tool for Clojure. I'll be diving into what it can do in a later chapter, but for now all you need to know is that it has a built-in REPL that we can (and will) use. Please refer to the Leiningen website[7] for the latest instructions for how to install it.

Just to reiterate, we'll be working exclusively from a terminal shell throughout the book in order for us to be able to utilize the Leiningen REPL.

For me, on a Mac, I use the Homebrew[8] package manager, as I find it to be the easiest option for installing Leiningen. With Homebrew installed, you can install Leiningen with the command seen in Listing 1-2.

Listing 1-2. Install Leining via Homebrew

```
brew install leiningen
```

Once installed, to start REPL, run the command lein repl. You should now see output that resembles Listing 1-3.

Listing 1-3. Output from Starting the Leiningen REPL

```
Retrieving org/clojure/tools.nrepl/0.2.12/tools.nrepl-0.2.12.pom from
central
Retrieving org/clojure/pom.contrib/0.1.2/pom.contrib-0.1.2.pom from central
Retrieving org/sonatype/oss/oss-parent/7/oss-parent-7.pom from central
Retrieving clojure-complete/clojure-complete/0.2.4/clojure-complete-
0.2.4.pom from clojars
Retrieving org/clojure/clojure/1.8.0/clojure-1.8.0.pom from central
Retrieving org/clojure/tools.nrepl/0.2.12/tools.nrepl-0.2.12.jar from
central
Retrieving org/clojure/clojure/1.8.0/clojure-1.8.0.jar from central
Retrieving clojure-complete/clojure-complete/0.2.4/clojure-complete-
0.2.4.jar from clojars

nREPL server started on port 55415 on host 127.0.0.1 -
nrepl://127.0.0.1:55415
REPL-y 0.3.7, nREPL 0.2.12
Clojure 1.8.0
Java HotSpot(TM) 64-Bit Server VM 1.8.0_92-b14
    Docs: (doc function-name-here)
          (find-doc "part-of-name-here")
```

---

[7]http://leiningen.org/
[8]http://brew.sh/

```
 Source: (source function-name-here)
Javadoc: (javadoc java-object-or-class-here)
   Exit: Control+D or (exit) or (quit)
Results: Stored in vars *1, *2, *3, an exception in *e

user=>
```

We can see from Listing 1-3 that Leiningen downloaded some dependencies for us (such as the Clojure language release 1.8.0). But you should also take note of the last line of the output: user=>.

The last line indicates that the namespace your code is going to be running within will be the user namespace. We'll be covering how namespaces work in a later chapter, but for now it'll suffice to know that Clojure allows you to segregate your code into namespaces to help isolate specific functionality (much like you would split files across separate folders).

One other thing to mention is that if you already have Java installed you can access a REPL without the need to download/install Leiningen. First, you would need to download and unzip Clojure. While in a terminal shell, you would execute the command shown in Listing 1-4.

Listing 1-4. Start a REPL Utilizing Java Directly

```
java -cp clojure-1.8.0.jar clojure.main
```

Listing 1-4 demonstrates how by using the Java command directly you can start up a Clojure REPL interface similar to what you'll see provided by Leiningen. But there are also online testers for when you're in a hurry:

- http://www.tryclj.com/

- http://himera.herokuapp.com/index.html (ClojureScript)

Now that we are within the Leiningen REPL environment, let's type something into it and see what happens. Try typing the code shown in Listing 1-5 and see if the output matches your expectations (I know we've not learned the Clojure syntax yet, but I'm hoping that the code will describe itself well enough for you to have a vague idea of the result before I explain it):

Listing 1-5. Execute Some Basic Clojure Code

```
(+ 2 2)
```

Once you type into the REPL the code from Listing 1-5 and hit the ENTER key, you should see the result of this line of code being executed. If you've typed the code correctly, you will see the result is 4.

Throughout the book, I will encourage you to try out the different code examples by typing them into the REPL, as this is the best way to experiment with and learn the language.

■ **Note**   Comments in Clojure code are denoted by a semi-colon ;, and a common convention in Clojure is to use two semi-colons.

OK, so this was a nice and simple snippet of code to try out. But what does this code actually represent? Well, in the next chapter we'll begin to learn the basic syntax for Clojure and peek at some of its data structures, but before we do that, let's finish up by reviewing one last important subject. . .

Documentation

If at any time you'd like to look up a function, then the quickest way to do that is within the REPL itself by using the doc function.

For example, if I wanted to remind myself how to increment a number using the inc function in Clojure, I would go to the REPL and execute the code seen in Listing 1-6.

Listing 1-6. Look Up Documentation for the inc Function

```
(doc inc)
```

This would return back to me the output seen in Listing 1-7.

Listing 1-7. Documentation for the inc Function

```
clojure.core/inc
([x])
  Returns a number one greater than num. Does not auto-promote
  longs, will throw on overflow. See also: inc'
nil
```

From this output, the first thing we can see is the namespace in which the function is located (clojure.core/inc). We'll be covering namespaces in a lot of detail within a later chapter, but it's worth noting now that Clojure has a core namespace that provides a standardized set of functions you can use.

We can also see that the function inc takes a single argument (that's what the [x] is indicating), and we can also read the description provided to get a better understanding of the context of the function (i.e., what its purpose is).

Clojure "namespaces" are a way to divide your code up into separate files. The primary namespace in Clojure is the clojure.core namespace. If you need to view the documentation for a function that isn't part of clojure.core, then you'll need to include the namespace when using the doc function within the REPL. For example, if you wanted to look up the blank? function, which is located within the clojure.string namespace, then in the REPL you would execute (doc clojure.string/blank?).

For Java documentation (which you sometimes need to do, as Clojure piggybacks off Java libraries on occasion), you'll need to use the javadoc function instead of doc. For example, if we wanted to look up the Formatter class in Java (which is found in Java's util namespace), we'd execute the code you see in Listing 1-8.

Listing 1-8. Look Up Documentation for a Java Class

```
(javadoc java.util.Formatter)
```

Executing the code within Listing 1-8 would open the relevant Java documentation in your web browser instead of loading the results within the terminal. This isn't as nice as looking up Clojure-specific functionality, but it's very rare that you would need to look up Java when writing Clojure (maybe you would look through a stack trace in your code and would be interested in learning more about the class that was referenced).

Summary

So, at this point we know a little bit about the background of Clojure and how to execute code within a REPL. In the next chapter, we'll start exploring some of the data structures that Clojure provides. These structures help us to achieve much more practical things with the Clojure language.

CHAPTER 2

■ ■ ■

Data Structures and Syntax

Clojure provides a language API based upon a select set of data structures. What this means is that the syntax for certain programming functionality matches the underlying data structures.

For example, here are the main data structures that Clojure provides:

- List: (1 2 3)
- Vector: [1 2 3]
- Map: {:foo "bar"}
- Set: #{1 2 3}

■ **Note** There are other data structures, terminology, and related concepts, as well as a great reference guide, which can be found in the official Clojure documentation.[1] However, for the purposes of what we wish to cover in this chapter, it can be a little "low-level" at times, as it also discusses some of the underlying Java interfaces that Clojure utilizes.

Clojure's data structures are read-only (also referred to as being immutable), meaning that when you make a change to the values stored within the data structure, a new version of the data structure is returned. We'll come back to this concept later on.

All data structures can be mixed and nested. See Listing 2-1.

Listing 2-1. Example of Nested Data Structures

```
[1 2 [3 {:name "Mark"}]]
```

■ **Note** You'll see that there are no delimiters between individual elements. You can add them if you want, but they're optional, and idiomatic Clojure code will typically omit them (e.g., [1 2 3] can be written as [1, 2, 3]).

---

[1]https://clojure.org/reference/data_structures

© Mark McDonnell 2017
M. McDonnell, *Quick Clojure*, DOI 10.1007/978-1-4842-2952-1_2

You can also refer to all these data structures as *sequences*. A sequence is an interface defined by Clojure, which allows multiple data structures that support the interface to share access to a set of built-in functions. We'll cover the topic of sequences in more detail in a later chapter.

There are many functions available within the Clojure programming language that are actually designed to work with multiple types of data structures. This isn't something you see in many other languages, and consequently it affords us some great flexibility and adaptability in our code.

Let's now review each of these data structures in a little more depth and see which functions we can use from Clojure's core library to manipulate them. We'll start with the list data structure, as that has the most complexity around it.

List

In order to appreciate the importance of the list data structure in a language such as Clojure, we need to understand that Clojure is a dialect of Lisp, which stands for "LISt Processing". Lisp is both a programming language (originally designed in 1958) and also a recognised structural basis for a collection of programming languages (Common Lisp, Scheme and Clojure being a few popular examples of languages that are built upon the same syntax as Lisp).

In simplistic terms, a language can be considered a dialect of lisp when it implements a parenthesized prefix notation syntax. This type of notation is distinct in that parentheses are used to group logic, and within the parentheses operators are placed to the left of their operands.

In a practical sense, when looking at a language such as Clojure, prefix notation means that inside the parentheses a function to be executed is what's specified first, followed by any arguments that function accepts. If we look at the list data structure, we can see that the syntax is the same as prefix notation. This is why the list data structure is prevalent across all Lisp languages, as it was a fundamental part of the original language design.

A list uses parentheses as its surrounding delimiters, and so an empty list would look like ( ), whereas a list with three elements could look like ("a" "b" "c").

The power of a Lisp based language (such as Clojure) comes from the fact that the language API utilizes the same syntax as the underlying data structures it manipulates. This is unlike other languages, whose API design is usually a lot of syntactic sugar on top of the underlying data structures they manipulate.

This mimicry between API syntax and the underlying data structures allows the Clojure programming language to rewrite itself and implement additional features it was not initially designed for (we'll see how this can be achieved later on when we learn about Clojure's Macros feature). But in essence this concept is what is meant by the word *homoiconic*: "code is data", as mentioned at the beginning of Chapter 1.

Now that you recognize how a programming interface for a Lisp-based language uses the same syntax as the underlying data structures, you'll likely have noticed that Clojure's syntax for executing a function also happens to be a list data structure. For example, (+ 1 2) is a function call that produces the result of 1 + 2, but (+ 1 2) is also itself a list data structure.

When Clojure evaluates the text (+ 1 2), it tokenizes the individual parts and evaluates them. In this instance, it is being provided a list data structure, and when provided this particular data structure, the Clojure language interpreter expects the first element within that structure to be a function and the remaining elements to be arguments that are passed to the function.

So, in our example we provided the + function and two arguments. The first argument was the value 1, and the second argument was the value 2. We'll learn more about functions later on, but for now you should know that the syntax structure for *calling* a function is as shown in Listing 2-2.

Listing 2-2. Syntax Structure for Calling a Function

```
(fn arg1 arg2 arg3...)
```

■ **Note**   When using the REPL, you might not realize it, but the `clojure.core` namespace (and all the functions it contains) have been pre-loaded for you. This is where the + function has come from. We will cover namespaces in a later chapter.

In Clojure a list is implemented as a linked list,[2] which means if you want to loop through its contents you'll have to start from the beginning of the list and move next, next, next until you reach the end of the list. This is the essence of how a linked list data structure works.

A list is very efficient at putting new elements onto the beginning of itself, but isn't very good at putting new elements onto the end of itself. This is because if it's a very long list, then it could take some time to step through each element in the list trying to find the end.

Now, most of the time when programming in Clojure, you shouldn't have to worry about how certain data structures are implemented "under the covers." Clojure will happily hide those details away from you and provide abstractions that make dealing with data structures in the most appropriate and performant manner very easy.

That being said, I personally feel it's important we know what implementation sits underneath a data structure, because it allows us to make decisions that can result in optimized code performance (when we really need it). It also means we won't be left scratching our heads trying to understand why a certain function didn't provide the result we were expecting.

If you need to add a value onto a linked list data structure, then you have a couple of options. You can be explicit about your understanding of the underlying implementation of the list (i.e., you now know a list data structure is implemented as a linked list) by using the cons function, which will insert your value at the beginning of the list, as shown in Listing 2-3.

Listing 2-3. Using cons to Be Explicit About Data-Structure Manipulation

```
(cons 4 '(1 2 3))

;; (4 1 2 3)
```

Or, you can use an abstraction like the conj function instead, which will pick the correct method for inserting the new value depending on the underlying data structure. So, for example, if your data structure is a list (which is implemented as a linked list), then conj will place the value at the start of the list, as shown in Listing 2-4.

---

[2]http://en.wikipedia.org/wiki/Linked_list

Listing 2-4. Using the conj Abstraction Function on a List

```
(conj '(1 2 3) 4)

;; (4 1 2 3)
;; same as the more explicit cons
```

But, if your data structure were a vector collection instead (and we'll look at vectors in the next section), then the conj function would know to insert the value at the end of the collection (which is more performant when dealing with vectors), as seen in Listing 2-5.

Listing 2-5. Using the conj Abstraction Function on a Vector

```
(conj [1 2 3] 4)

;; [1 2 3 4]
```

Some readers may be wondering about the single quote in front of the list data structure (i.e., '(1 2 3)); we'll discuss this in more detail when we talk about Macros in Clojure, but effectively it prevents Clojure from evaluating the list as if it was a function and instead allows Clojure to treat it as a *literal* list data structure.

Otherwise, without the single quote, as we mentioned earlier, Clojure would try to execute the list as if the first argument were a function; so, it would attempt to locate and execute a function by the identifier 1 and pass it the values 2 and 3 as arguments to the function. But there is no such function called 1, and so an error would occur.

The list data structure is the only structure where you have to worry about quoting. Alternatively, you can use the list function to dynamically create the list. For example, (cons 4 (list 1 2 3)).

There are other abstraction functions (like conj), such as peek and pop, which help to determine the right "process" for the data structures they're being applied to. See Listing 2-6.

Listing 2-6. The peek and pop Abstraction Functions

```
(peek [1 2 3])  ;; 3
(peek '(1 2 3)) ;; 1

(pop [1 2 3])  ;; [1 2]
(pop '(1 2 3)) ;; (2 3)
```

Notice how the peek and pop methods handle things differently depending on the data structure being provided. It knows that a list (i.e., '(1 2 3)) is a linked list, and so it handles things from the beginning of the data structure, whereas it knows a vector (i.e., [1 2 3]) has "index access," and so it's more performant at working from the end of the data structure.

Vector

Chances are your current programming language will have a data structure that resembles a vector. In most other languages it is referred to as an array (although there are subtle semantic and implementation differences). Vectors allow you to have index access to any element within the data structure.

As an example, let's imagine we have a vector of five elements and we want to retrieve the fourth element. See Listing 2-7.

Listing 2-7. Demonstrate Index Access on a Vector Data Structure

```
(get [1 2 3 4 5] 3)

;; 4
```

As you can see, vectors are zero-indexed, so asking for 3 returns the fourth element. You could also use the nth function instead of get. The difference is that the latter (get) works across all types of collections (including maps and sets), whereas nth only works with vectors and lists.

You can modify the vector by using the assoc function (which is an abbreviation of "associate"). The way it works is that you provide the index of the vector you want to modify and then provide the value (see Listing 2-8).

Listing 2-8. Associate a Value into a Vector

```
(assoc [1 2 3 4 5] 5 6)

;; [1 2 3 4 5 6]
```

In the preceding example, we're saying "put into index 5 the value 6." Remember that vectors are zero-indexed, so our new value 6 will effectively be added to the end of the vector (as there currently is no fifth index).

■ **Note** If you want to add a value to the collection without specifying an index, then use conj, as demonstrated earlier.

Adding a value is cool, but what if you want to remove a value? One way to do this would be to use the pop function, which returns a copy of the vector but with the last element removed. See Listing 2-9, for example.

Listing 2-9. Return Copy of Vector with Last Item Removed

```
(pop [1 2 3 4 5])

;; [1 2 3 4]
```

So, what if you want to remove elements from the middle of a vector? Well, you should be aware that this requires a surprisingly complex number of steps when using a Lisp-based language such as Clojure.

You should also be aware that a vector probably isn't the best data structure to use if you plan on removing elements from the middle of it. For situations like that, where you want to manipulate the data in complex ways, you'll probably want to use a hash map instead (see the "Map" section after this for details).

Before we look at how to remove an item from the middle of a vector, let's first start with something similar but easier to achieve. Imagine you want to sample some of your data. You can do that by retrieving a "slice" of your vector. For example, if the vector looked like [1 2 3 4 5] and you wanted back a contiguous sample such as [2 3], you could use the subvec function, as shown in Listing 2-10.

Listing 2-10. Use subvec for Retrieving a Slice of Data

```
(subvec [1 2 3 4 5] 1 3)
```

In Listing 2-10, the code describes "starting from index 1 (which is the value 2 in the given vector), give me a copy from here *until* index 3," and so we get back that specific range [2 3].

■ **Note** We'll see later that there are many more functions for working with sequences/collections, and that because of the sequence abstraction that Clojure implements we can utilize these functions across different data structures.

Going back to the earlier point about how to remove an element from the middle of a vector, the code snippet in Listing 2-11 demonstrates how you could remove the number 3 from the collection [1 2 3 4 5] using subvec, leaving you with [1 2 4 5] as the resulting vector.

Now, it's important to realize that I'm about to demonstrate a rather inelegant solution. But once you're more familiar with Clojure and the available functions, you'll see this could easily be cleaned up. I'm also going to expand the already inelegant solution across multiple lines for readability.

Listing 2-11. Use subvec for Retrieving a Slice of Data

```
(vec
  (concat
    (subvec [1 2 3 4 5] 0 2)
    (subvec [1 2 3 4 5] 3)))
```

So, the way this works is we use subvec to take a slice from either end of the vector. So (subvec [1 2 3 4 5] 0 2) returns [1 2] while (subvec [1 2 3 4 5] 3) returns [4 5]. We then use the concat function to concatenate the two vectors together. Finally, because concat returns a list data structure, we use the vec function to convert the returned list back into a vector.

The fact that the concat function returns a list and not a vector isn't really an issue, because of how Clojure is able to handle collections as abstractions. But, in some cases it can be useful to ensure the returned data structure is in a specific format so you can take advantage of particular performance benefits.

I didn't have to worry about that for this basic example. I only converted the result back into a vector type in my example so as to avoid causing confusion when the result type came back different from what we provided.

We'll discuss why the change from a vector to a list happens in a later chapter, but for now it'll suffice to know that the reason we don't need to worry too much about the conversion between collection types is because of a concept known as the "Sequence Abstraction."

A more flexible and reusable solution would be to create a function that can wrap its complex implementation logic. The following example code, shown in Listing 2-12, is a much more flexible solution, and its logic is being wrapped up inside our own user-defined function, which we'll name drop-nth.

The function signature for our function will be (drop-nth <n> <collection>), and an example call would be (drop-nth 3 [:a :b :c :d]). The expected result would be that the third element (:c) in the vector is removed.

Before I demonstrate the implementation of our custom drop-nth function, I would suggest that if you're new to programming and/or Clojure, maybe skip ahead to the next section: "Map."

The following example is provided so that I can demonstrate how you might solve the earlier problem of needing to remove an element from the middle of a vector. But the solution does utilize a few different advanced features of the Clojure language. I recommend you continue reading on and come back to this example later once you've had a chance to learn more about the Clojure features this solution utilizes.

Listing 2-12. Remove Element from the Middle of a Vector

```
(defn drop-nth [n coll]
  (->> coll
    (map vector (iterate inc 1))
    (remove #(zero? (mod (first %) n)))
    (map second)))

(drop-nth 3 [:a :b :c :d])

;; (:a :b :d)
```

So, I'm going to attempt to break down this example, but again, don't worry too much at this point about really understanding the moving pieces, as we'll learn about each of these features in later chapters.

The first thing to mention is the use of ->>. This looks like a function, but strictly speaking it's actually a macro. The macro's name is the "thread last macro." Although the name includes the word *thread*, the macro has nothing to do with concurrency or multi-threaded code (which is a topic related to both multiple tasks overlapping as well as multiple tasks executed at the same time, and is something we'll cover in a lot of detail in a later chapter).

The macro ->> passes the value (in this case coll) as the last argument to each form listed within the call.

■ **Note**   In Clojure a "form" is basically an "expression," which is valid code that can be *evaluated* to produce a value.

So, the collection [:a :b :c :d] is passed into the drop-nth function as the argument/symbol coll and is also passed as the last argument to (map vector (iterate inc 1)). This means that once Clojure has compiled the form/expression, it'll end up looking something like (map vector (iterate inc 1) coll).

The result of the previous map form is itself then passed as the last argument to (remove #(zero? (mod (first %) n))).

OK, so that last form looks quite complicated. We can see that we're calling a function called remove, but what's all the stuff after it being passed as an argument? Well, that's an "anonymous" function.

When we defined our drop-nth function, we gave it the name drop-nth. But functions don't *need* a name in order to be executable, and so for convenience, instead of defining a function that will exist for the lifetime of the program, we've defined an inline/anonymous function for the purpose of doing a quick bit of processing and passing that result as the first argument to the remove function.

So, looking back at that form, we can see that it's really just calling the remove function and passing it two arguments: the first being an anonymous function #(zero? (mod (first %) n)) and the second being the result of the previous map form (which you don't *explicitly* see being passed as the second argument, thanks to the ->> macro).

Finally, the result of the previous remove form is passed as the last argument to (map second). If we didn't have the thread-last macro, then we'd be forced to write the (more complex) set of nested forms shown in Listing 2-13 (notice the order of the functions are now reversed, and it's written "outside-in").

Listing 2-13. Solution Without the Use of the Thread-Last Macro

```
(defn drop-nth [n coll]
  (map second
    (remove #(zero? (mod (first %) n))
      (map vector (iterate inc 1) coll))))

(drop-nth 3 [:a :b :c :d])

;; (:a :b :d)
```

Now, ultimately what we're aiming to do is to wrap all of this complex logic inside a user-defined function called drop-nth, meaning it is ready to be reused wherever we have the need to remove an item from a collection.

The underlying principle of how the preceding code works is that the collection you provide is turned into a structure that resembles (slightly) a hash map (something we'll look at in the next section, "Map").

So, for example, the collection [:a :b :c :d] would be converted into something like ([1 :a] [2 :b] [3 :c] [4 :d]). You can try this yourself in the REPL (see Listing 2-14).

Listing 2-14. Convert Collection into One with Numerical Access

```
(map vector (iterate inc 1) [:a :b :c :d])

;; ([1 :a] [2 :b] [3 :c] [4 :d])
```

I'll explain how the map function works in the next chapter, but for now it'll suffice to know that it loops over a given collection and passes each item in the collection to a function that can mutate the value. This now gives us a numerical hook into a particular element within the collection.

The next line, (remove #(zero? (mod (first %) n))), is a call to the remove function. We now know that we're passing the result of an anonymous function. The anonymous function is executing the predicate function zero?.

■ **Note** A "predicate" sounds more complicated than it really is. A predicate is simply a function that returns true or false.

The argument passed to zero? is an item from the collection ([1 :a] [2 :b] [3 :c] [4 :d]). The remove function executes zero? against each element in the provided collection. You can try this yourself by combining the preceding snippet with the output from the previous snippet, as shown in Listing 2-15.

Listing 2-15. Remove Item from Collection Based on Anonymous Function

```
(remove #(zero? (mod (first %) 3))
  '([1 :a] [2 :b] [3 :c] [4 :d]))

;; ([1 :a] [2 :b] [4 :d])
```

In Listing 2-15, you'll notice that I swapped what was n in our drop-nth implementation for the value 3. I did that just for the purposes of demonstrating how this extracted snippet of code works. I also needed to quote the list '(...) in the snippet; otherwise, it would have caused an error.

If you wanted, you could also have tried it with the original expression included instead of using the quoted '([1 :a] [2 :b] [3 :c] [4 :d]). See Listing 2-16.

Listing 2-16. Remove Item from Collection Using Original Form

```
(remove #(zero? (mod (first %) 3))
  (map vector (iterate inc 1) [:a :b :c :d]))

;; ([1 :a] [2 :b] [4 :d])
```

OK, we've diverted from our focus a bit there. Going back to what we were saying before, the first element is [1 :a], and in this case the anonymous function is able to access that via the % symbol. It retrieves the number 1 and divides it by n (and in the preceding example this was the number 3 that was originally passed as an argument to drop-nth). It does this calculation to verify if the numbers divide evenly; if they do, then zero will be the result and the predicate (which is the zero? function) will return true, meaning that the element should be removed from the collection.

The only element in the collection that can divide evenly and result in a modulus of zero would be [3 :c]. This means the overall result of the remove function is ([1 :a] [2 :b] [4 :d]).

Now, we've successfully removed the requested element. But we still need to convert our data structure back to its original form. To do this, we move to the final line of the function (map second), which maps over the resulting collection, which is still a collection of sub vectors—([1 :a] [2 :b] [4 :d])—and returns a modified version where it has removed the first element from each nested collection by specifically retrieving the "second" item.

So, the first nested collection is [1 :a], meaning (map second) will remove the 1 and leave :a. The overall function result is (:a :b :d), which is what we desired originally, the ability to remove a specific element from the collection that wasn't the start or end position.

Now, one concern with the current drop-nth implementation is that it will actually remove *every* nth item. So, if you executed (drop-nth 3 [:a :b :c :d :e :f :g :h :i :j]), then the result would be (:a :b :d :e :g :h :j). Notice it didn't just remove the third item, but rather every third item. This might not necessarily be what you wanted to have happen.

The solution, remembering the problem was removing a *single* value from the middle of a collection, is to replace #(zero? (mod (first %) n)) with #(= (first %) n), which causes all other iterations to fail because only 3 will be "equal" to the third element (notice we replaced the zero? predicate with the = function).

Before we move on, instead of using remove we could have used another function called filter instead (I demonstrate filter in the following chapter), but I think semantically remove makes more sense. The only difference between the two functions is in the use of the predicate.

The filter function will keep elements if its predicate returns true (the semantics of the function are "filter out elements I want"). The remove function will keep elements if its predicate returns false (the semantics of the function are "remove elements that pass the test").

Map

The map data structure goes by many different names—hash, hash map, dictionary—and what distinguishes it from other data structures is the underlying implementation, which is a key part of ensuring the algorithmic performance of this particular data structure (but that topic of discussion is outside the scope of this book).

Effectively, a map is a key/value lookup. You provide a key and associate a value with that key. See Listing 2-17, for example.

Listing 2-17. Simple Map Data Structure

```
{:my-key "this is my value"}
```

■ **Note**   Clojure maps have a 1:1 mapping to JSON.

We use the get function to retrieve a value for a specified key, as seen in Listing 2-18.

Listing 2-18. Retrieve Value from a Map Data Structure

```
(get {:my-key "this is my value"} :my-key)

;; "this is my value"
```

■ **Note**   If you want the entire entry (i.e., the key and the value, not just the value) then you can use find instead:

(find {:a 1 :b 2} :a) will return [:a 1]

We can also add a key to an existing map using the assoc function. We used assoc earlier with the vector data structure, so already you can see the "Sequence Abstraction" coming into play with a function that can be used consistently across different data structure types. See Listing 2-19.

Listing 2-19. Associate a New Key/Value Pair into a Map Data Structure

```
(assoc {:foo "bar"} :baz "qux")

;; {:foo "bar", :baz "qux"}
```

You can also remove pairs using the dissoc function, like in Listing 2-20.

Listing 2-20. Remove a Key/Value Pair from a Map Data Structure

```
(dissoc {:foo "bar" :baz "qux"} :baz)

;; {:foo "bar"}
```

Similarly, if you need to return a new map that consists of a *specific* key, then you can use the select-keys function, shown in Listing 2-21.

Listing 2-21. Filter Map for Specific Keys

```
(select-keys {:name "Mark" :age 33 :location "London"} [:name :location])

;; {:name "Mark", :location "London"}
```

You'll notice in the preceding example that the returned map is now correctly missing the :age key pair. Also, take note of the fact that unlike dissoc, where you can specify multiple keys as arguments in order to remove them all from the resulting map, with select-keys you need to specify multiple keys within a vector in order to select the pairs you want.

Keywords

Some readers may be wondering what the colon prefixing the key is supposed to mean (i.e., as we've seen with :foo and :baz). The colon indicates that the key is actually a *keyword*. If you've used Symbols in Ruby, then it's the same thing. If not, then know that its usage is primarily for performance reasons.

To elaborate, if you create a map key with a string (e.g., {"my-key" "my key value"}), then every time you reference the key using a string, you'll be recreating it in memory, whereas referencing a key via a keyword is only done once.

To understand this better, imagine we have the vector seen in Listing 2-22 with the same value for every element.

Listing 2-22. Demonstrate Keyword Performance

```
["hi" "hi" "hi"]

;; creates the string "hi" three times in memory

[:hi :hi :hi]

;; the value hi is created once in memory
```

So, we can see the performance benefit of specifying a keyword once and having the underlying memory allocation reused wherever the keyword is found in the code. This is why you'll see keywords used the majority of the time instead of a string (unless you have a very specific need for a string).

■ **Note**   You can convert a string into a keyword using the keyword function: (keyword "my-string"), which returns :my-string. The reverse is also possible with the name function: (name :my-string), which returns "my-string".

There is one important addition to the use of keywords—if you use them as keys inside a map, then the keyword acts like a get function.

So, for example, imagine you have a map {:foo "bar" :baz "qux"} and you wanted the value from the :baz key. You could use either of the following snippets seen in Listing 2-23 to get at that value.

Listing 2-23. Keyword as a Function

```
(get {:foo "bar" :baz "qux"} :baz)

;; "qux"

(:baz {:foo "bar" :baz "qux"})
;; "qux"
```

In Listing 2-23 we've used the familiar get function like before to retrieve the value of the specified key, but we can also just use the keyword in the place where a function is expected, and it'll return the value for that key. If you're unsure whether your map includes a certain key, then you can use the contains? function, as seen in Listing 2-24.

Listing 2-24. Demonstrate the contains? Function

```
(contains? {:foo "bar" :baz "qux"} :foo)

;; true
```

Keys, Values, and Replacement

Before we finish up with looking at the map data structure, let's take a moment to review a few simpler functions (keys, vals, and replace), as well as to understand what a *struct* is. First, let's see the keys/vals functions and how they work (Listing 2-25).

Listing 2-25. Demonstrate the keys and vals Functions

```
(keys {:foo "bar" :baz "qux"})
;; (:baz :foo)

(vals {:foo "bar" :baz "qux"})
;; ("qux" "bar")
```

As you can see in Listing 2-25, with keys we pass the function a map data structure and it returns all the keys specified within the data structure. The vals function is similar in that we pass it a map data structure, but this time it returns just the values assigned to each key.

The replace function allows you to create a new vector consisting of values extracted from a map data structure. It does this by using the key name for the value you want to extract. So, if you had the following map {:a 1 :b 2 :c 3} and you wanted to generate the vector [3 2 1], then you could do that with the code in Listing 2-26.

Listing 2-26. Demonstrate the replace Function

```
(replace {:a 1 :b 2 :c 3} [:c :b :a])
```

■ **Note**   The replace function works on vectors, but using index values rather than keys:

```
(replace [:a :b :c] [2 1 0]) will return [:c :b :a].
```

Finally, let's understand what structs are in Clojure. Effectively, they are a simple way to generate maps from a predefined structure. So, for example, if I wanted a map data structure that resembled attributes of a person, then I could manually execute the code seen in Listing 2-27.

Listing 2-27. Assign Map Structures to Identifiable Symbols

```
(def mark {:name "Mark" :age 35})
(def rich {:name "Richard" :age 40})
(def cat {:name "Catherine" :age 30})
```

■ **Note**   The use of the def function is so we can declare a variable. We'll come back to variables in a little while, but, in short, they define a location in memory where data can be stored; we can then refer back to that data using the variable's name.

In the preceding example, you'll notice that there is a lot of duplication with regards to my typing the keys :name and :age (and realistically there would be many more attributes I'd want to record). This can be wasted time and adds the potential for typo errors to cause annoying bugs, never mind the inconsistency of adding new keys to one of the maps and forgetting to add them to the other maps as well.

It would be better for us to abstract away the "structure" of the map so that we can focus on just providing the data, and that's where the create-struct and struct functions come in handy, as seen in Listing 2-28.

Listing 2-28. Demonstrate create-struct and struct Functions

```
(def person (create-struct :name :age :sex))

(struct person "Mark" 35 "Male")
;; {:name "Mark", :age 35, :sex "Male"}

(struct person "Richard" 40 "Male")
;; {:name "Richard", :age 40, :sex "Male"}

(struct person "Catherine" 30 "Female")
;; {:name "Catherine", :age 30, :sex "Female"}
```

■ **Note**   Clojure provides a shortcut by way of a macro called `defstruct`. This macro handles the creation of structs and storing them in a variable. So, instead of `(def person (create-struct :name :age :sex))`, you could use `(defstruct person :name :age :sex)`.

Set

A set is a data structure made up of unique values. Much like Clojure's map and vector data structures, it provides Clojure with a very lightweight data model. The example in Listing 2-29 is what a set typically looks like.

Listing 2-29. Simple Set Data Structure Example

```
#{1 2 3 :a :b :c}

;; #{1 :c 3 2 :b :a}
```

The order of a set is not guaranteed (as seen in the preceding example's return value). Although you can create a sorted set by using the `sorted-set` function, be warned you can't use mixed-types with a sorted set. See Listing 2-30.

Listing 2-30. Simple Set Data Structure Example

```
(sorted-set 3 1 2)
;; #{1 2 3}

(sorted-set 1 2 3 :a :b :c)
;; error - mixed types
```

If you already have a set created and it's unsorted, then you can use the `apply` function (which works for any collection type: lists, vectors, maps, and sets) to apply the `sorted-set` function onto the existing set, like in Listing 2-31.

Listing 2-31. Apply sorted-set onto Existing Set

```
(apply sorted-set #{3 1 2})

;; #{1 2 3}
```

The ability to apply with a sorted-set can come in handy when dealing with existing collections, because you can filter out duplicates at the same time as sorting them, as in Listing 2-32.

Listing 2-32. Filter Out Duplicates

```
(set [1 1 2 2 3 3 4 5 6 6])

;; #{1 4 6 3 2 5}

(apply sorted-set [1 1 2 2 3 3 4 5 6 6])

;; #{1 2 3 4 5 6}
```

You can also use the conj function to add a new value to the set, but remember that a set is a collection of unique values, and so if you try to add a value that already exists, it'll be quietly ignored. See Listing 2-33.

Listing 2-33. Using conj to Add New Value to a Set

```
(conj #{1 2 3} 4)

;; #{1 4 3 2}

(conj #{1 2 3} 3)

;; #{1 3 2}
```

Lastly, being able to add items to a set is wonderful, but being able to remove items is equally useful at times, and we do this using disj (see Listing 2-34).

Listing 2-34. Remove Items from a Set with disj

```
(disj #{1 2 3} 3)

;; #{1 2}
```

Vars and Symbols

OK, this is the last bit of basic syntax I want to cover before moving on. In this section, I want to demonstrate not only how variables work (you'll be very familiar with this concept from other programming languages), but also how symbols tie into variables and the use of the def function along with the defn macro.

Let's start by understanding what a symbol is. A symbol, in its simplest form, is a reference to some other value. It's an identity of sorts, like your name; it identifies *you*, and although you change over time (you get older, right?) your identity stays the same.

A variable, on the other hand, is a mutable storage location. When creating a variable, it is created within the current namespace (this prevents conflicts with other namespaces). To create a variable in Clojure, you need to use the def function so you can assign the value to a symbol. See Listing 2-35.

Listing 2-35. Using def to Assign a Value to a Symbol/Variable

```
(def foo "hello")
```

In Listing 2-35, I've called the def function and passed the symbol foo and the string "hello" as arguments. The def function associates the symbol foo with the string "hello" so that when I type the symbol foo into the REPL (within the current namespace), it'll know where to go to look up the value and return me the value associated with the symbol (which in this case would be the value "hello").

■ **Note**   Internally, Clojure manages a global map of namespaces and their associated variables.

Variables are not available within other namespaces unless they are "interned" into them. *Interning* is a fancy way of saying "find variable x within this current namespace; and if it doesn't exist then create it." But you can also "intern" variables from another namespace using the :refer feature of the ns macro. I'll demonstrate how that works in a later chapter, when we look in more detail at namespaces.

Assigning Functions

Now, variables don't just contain single values (strings or data structures, etc.); they can also be assigned functions. For example, Listing 2-36 shows a variable that creates a function that says hello to you (you would probably have a short function like this written all on one line, but I've opened it up across multiple lines for readability).

Listing 2-36. Assign a Function to a Variable

```
(def foo
  (fn [p]
    (prn
      (str "Hello " p "!"))))
```

You also have the ability to define an anonymous function, which is a function that has no identifier, "inline" within an existing expression. We saw an example of this earlier in the chapter when dealing with the vector data structure (see Listing 2-38 below for a reminder of the syntax structure for an anonymous function). In Listing 2-36, we've defined a foo variable and assigned an "anonymous" function that takes p as an argument and then prints out a message using the prn function. We do this by taking the value of p and interpolating it into a single string value using the str function. You would call this function as shown in Listing 2-37.

Listing 2-37. Example of Calling Our User-Defined Function

```
(foo "you")

;; "Hello you!"
```

Listing 2-38. Syntax Structure of an Anonymous Function Definition

```
(fn [arg1 arg2 arg3...] (fn-body...))
```

In the earlier example (Listing 2-36), where we defined the foo function, we also were treated to a demonstration on how to nest function calls. So, we saw str nested inside of prn, and prn nested inside of fn, etc. We can see that Clojure is evaluating the "forms" from right to left.

■ **Note**   A *form* is something that is handed to the Clojure parser (i.e., Reader[3]). An example of a form could be a string or a symbol, or even a function (which contains forms inside it). You'll hear people mention forms a lot when talking about Clojure code, so you should be familiar with the terminology.

The Clojure parser evaluates the str function and passes the result to the prn function, which is then used as the function body. Now, defining a variable and assigning a function to it is such a common pattern that a macro was created within the core Clojure library to reduce the verbosity a little bit and make it easier to remember the syntax.

So, instead of the long-form def, you can use defn as shown in Listing 2-39 (again, I've expanded it over multiple lines for readability, but this could be a one- or two-liner at most).

Listing 2-39. Example of the defn Macro

```
(defn foo [p]
  (prn
    (str "Hello " p "!")))
```

Temp Variables

Creating temporary variables can be achieved via the let form. The way let works is that you use a *binding*. A binding is a fancy way of saying "assign a value to a symbol," and that symbol exists only while the let block is executed, after which it disappears. See Listing 2-40.

---

[3]https://clojure.org/reference/reader

Listing 2-40. Example `let` Binding

```
(let [xyz "Hi!"]
  (prn xyz))

;; nil

(prn xyz)

;; CompilerException java.lang.RuntimeException:
;; Unable to resolve symbol: xyz in this context
```

In Listing 2-40, we can see that the `let` binding prints "Hi!" as a side effect, but ultimately returns `nil`. Then, if we try to print the symbol `xyz` again from outside of the `let` binding, we see it raises an exception.

■ **Note**   Clojure also provides a feature called transients,[4] which is a way to create a non-persistent copy of a data structure. You can mutate this temporary structure and then use a call to `persistent!` to return a persistent/immutable version. This allows for some good performance enhancements when utilized in the right scenarios where temp structures are more performant.

We'll come back to `let` blocks later on when we discuss *destructuring*, which is a very powerful feature for extracting values from complex objects.

■ **Note**   Local variables created via `let` aren't *really* variables, as their values cannot be changed once set.

Dynamic Variables

When creating variables, they are bound to the current namespace and are marked as "static." But variables can be *dynamically* changed (for a temporary period of time). Similar to how `let` allows you to define local variables, the `binding` macro allows a current thread to manipulate the value of a variable while execution is happening within its block, like in Listing 2-41.

---

[4]https://clojure.org/reference/transients

Listing 2-41. Example of Dynamic Variable Bindings

```
(def ^:dynamic my-name "Mark")

(prn my-name) ;; "Mark"

(binding [my-name "Bob"]
  (prn my-name)) ;; "Bob"

(prn my-name) ;; "Mark"
```

As you can see from the preceding example, we've defined a variable my-name the same way as we've defined variables previously; the only difference is that we now have added the metadata ^:dynamic. Now, when using the binding form we can dynamically change the variable's value temporarily. You can see it reverts back once the block has finished.

This is particularly useful for testing purposes. Remember: functions can be assigned to variables too, so within a test environment you could dynamically swap out the function implementation. Clojure has since also implemented two additional functions, with-redefs[5] and with-redefs-fn,[6] specifically for this purpose.

You could also use this functionality to provide a style of programming known as aspect-oriented programming.[7] For example, you could manipulate a logging function so it placed context-specific details around the standard log information.

Summary

OK, we've covered a fair amount of ground here. Make sure you play around in the REPL with the examples given and see what happens when you tweak the examples (it's the best way to confirm your understanding of these concepts and the behavior we've discussed so far).

In the following chapter, we'll start to look at the concepts surrounding functional programming and how they are reflected in the Clojure language. This will include topics such as immutability, referential transparency, first-class functions, partial application, recursive iteration, and composability.

---

[5]http://clojure.github.io/clojure/clojure.core-api.html#clojure.core/with-redefs
[6]http://clojure.github.io/clojure/clojure.core-api.html#clojure.core/
with-redefs-fn
[7]https://en.wikipedia.org/wiki/Aspect-oriented_programming

CHAPTER 3

■ ■ ■

Functional Programming

Clojure is a functional language, so it provides certain features you would expect to find in other functional programming (FP) languages, such as the following:

- Immutability
- Referential transparency
- First-class functions
- Partial application
- Recursive iteration
- Composability

Let's take a moment to consider each of these features.

Immutability

The idea behind immutability is that it is used when we wish to avoid "mutating state." What that really means is that it helps us to avoid changing data that might be used by multiple (separate) areas of a program.

If you have state and it can change, then once your application becomes distributed and concurrent (i.e., multi-threaded), you'll end up in a world of hurt, as many different threads can start manipulating your data at non-deterministic times. This can cause your application to fail at any given moment and become very hard to debug and to reason about.

By offering immutability, Clojure can help to side-step this problem. In Clojure, every time you manipulate a data structure you are returned not a mutated version of the original, but rather a whole new copy with your change(s) applied.

■ **Note**   Having complete copies of your data might sound like a performance nightmare, but thanks to how Clojure implements certain data structures internally—using tries[1]—it's actually very efficient. Clojure calls this Persistent Data Structures.

---

[1]http://en.wikipedia.org/wiki/Trie

© Mark McDonnell 2017
M. McDonnell, *Quick Clojure*, DOI 10.1007/978-1-4842-2952-1_3

Immutability is a strange concept to grasp when coming from an object-oriented language (OOP). This is because functional programming (FP) and OOP have different goals.

OOP is about *encapsulating* data (state) and providing *controlled* access via object methods. FP is about the *flow* of a software system, where data is passed *through* a set of functions that manipulate the data as it makes its way out to the end user (i.e., the data is filtered).

Referential Transparency

Referential transparency is when an expression can be replaced by its value without changing the behavior of a program. In a practical sense, it's when you define a function that takes an argument and always returns the same value when given the same argument. See Listing 3-1.

■ **Note** There is a related concept called *pure functions* that more broadly refers to a function whose return value is determined by its inputs, and with no visible side effects.

Listing 3-1. Example of a Referentially Transparent Function

```
(defn sum [x y]
  (+ x y))

(sum 1 1)

;; 2
```

The function sum (shown in Listing 3-1) is referentially transparent. No matter what happens, if I provide the same set of arguments (in this case 1 and 1), I'll always get back the same result.

Every program needs state of some sort, and that's why Clojure is not a "strict" FP language like maybe Haskell.[2] Clojure's philosophy is to strive for being functional and referentially transparent wherever possible.

First-class Functions

For a language to offer "first-class functions," it needs to be able to both store functions and pass functions around as if they were values. We've already seen the former being achieved using variables, and the latter (passing functions around as values) is also possible within Clojure.

---

[2]https://www.haskell.org/

■ **Note**   The concept of first-class functions helps to promote the idea of *higher-order functions*. A higher-order function is one that can either take or return a function as a value. There are many higher-order functions in Clojure: map, reduce, comp, apply, partial, and filter, and I'll demonstrate all of these within this chapter.

Let's begin by seeing an—admittedly simple and silly— example of first-class functions in action (Listing 3-2).

Listing 3-2. Example of How Clojure Supports First-class Functions

```
(defn cap [s]
  (clojure.string/upper-case s))

(defn greeting [c s]
  (prn (c s)))

(greeting cap "hi there")

;; "HI THERE"
```

In Listing 3-2, we've defined a cap function, which we're passing in to a greeting function. This demonstrates how functions can be passed around as if they were values and meets the first half of the "first-class function" requirement.

■ **Note**   The cap function itself isn't important, but you'll see we've referenced a function clojure.string/upper-case. This is a "fully qualified" function, meaning we've given an explicit/direct path to where the function can be located (within the clojure.string namespace; we'll cover namespaces in a later chapter).

The other half of that requirement is the ability to return a function from a function (as opposed to returning a value from a function). We can see an example of this in Listing 3-3, where the partial function doesn't return a value but rather another function.

I'll demonstrate how partial application works in the following section, but hopefully the example in Listing 3-3 is simple enough to highlight the potential for what partial application can provide.

Listing 3-3. Example of Partial Application

```
(defn sum [x y]
  (+ x y))

(def add-on-five (partial sum 5))

(add-on-five 10)

;; 15
```

Other examples of Clojure's first-class function credentials can be found in the following list. In each of the subsequent examples, we'll demonstrate first-class functions by passing existing functions into other functions. The functions we'll be using in our examples are:

- complement
- apply
- map
- reduce
- filter
- comp

Complement

The complement function is very simple: it takes in a predicate and returns a predicate (remember that a *predicate* is what you call a function if it returns a Boolean value). See Listing 3-4.

Listing 3-4. Example of the complement function returning the opposite truth value

```
((complement empty?) "")

;; false
```

■ **Note**   The naming convention used for predicate functions is similar to the Ruby programming language in that you suffix a question mark onto the name of predicates (e.g., even?).

In our example, we pass an empty string into our new predicate function. The empty? function would normally return true for an empty string, but the point of complement is to *reverse* the original Boolean, so instead we get false.

For this example, to be more practical, you would ideally save the new predicate function in a variable called not-empty? to allow for maximum reusability.

Apply

The apply example takes a function (in this case it will be str, which concatenates strings together) and a collection ["a" "b" "c"] and then passes each element in the collection to the specified function.

Listing 3-5. Example of apply

```
(apply str ["a" "b" "c"])

;; "abc"
```

In Listing 3-5, we're able to utilize a collection, while the effect of this code is that it in essence works like we called (str "a" "b" "c") instead. The benefit of the apply function is for times when you don't know what the arguments will be until *runtime*.

Map

In the following example (Listing 3-6), we're using map to apply a function to the collection [1 2 3], which means we're able to increment each value within the collection by one, thanks to the use of the inc function.

Listing 3-6. Example of map

```
(map inc [1 2 3])

;; (2 3 4)
```

Be aware that if you use map over a map data structure (e.g., {:a 1 :b 2 :c 3}) you'll find you get returned a list data structure (and not necessarily in the order you expect). We see this in Listing 3-7.

Listing 3-7. The map Return Value Type Is a List

```
(map
  (fn [[k v]] (inc v))
  {:a 1 :b 2 :c 3}) ;; => (4 3 2)

;; (2 3 4)
```

So, you if you need a map data structure returned, make sure you construct the returning data structure in such a way that on the way out it resembles a key/value structure. Once we have this key/value-like data structure, we'll be able to convert it into an actual map data structure. Listing 3-8 demonstrates how you might do this.

Listing 3-8. Ensure map Returns Key/Value-like Data Structure

```
(map
  (fn [[k v]] [k (inc v)])
  {:a 1 :b 2 :c 3})

;; ([:c 4] [:b 3] [:a 2])
```

Now that we have our key/value-like structure ([:c 4] [:b 3] [:a 2]), we can wrap the preceding form with the into function to convert that returned structure (i.e., the list of sub-vectors) back into a map from a list, as in Listing 3-9.

Listing 3-9. Convert Key/Value-like Data Structure Back into a map Data Structure

```
(into {}
  (map
    (fn [[k v]] [k (inc v)])
    {:a 1 :b 2 :c 3}))

;; {:c 4, :b 3, :a 2}
```

Reduce

In Listing 3-10, we're using the reduce function, which accepts two arguments. The first is a function (this function must itself accept two arguments), and the second should be a collection. Reduce iterates over the given collection and passes each item through to the provided function (in Listing 3-10 we provide the + function and the collection [1 2 3]).

Listing 3-10. Example of the reduce Function

```
(reduce + [1 2 3 4])

;; 10
```

What's probably not obvious in this particular example is that reduce requires an *accumulator*, which is passed through as the first argument to the given function for each iteration. You can provide an initial value for an accumulator, but if you don't provide one then the first element in the collection is used.

We didn't provide an accumulator in the preceding example, and so the first item (1) was used as the initial accumulated value. This means 1 was given to the + function as the first argument, and the second item in the collection (2) was given to the + function as the second argument. The + function then added the two values together, which resulted in the value 3. That value was then provided as the accumulator on the next iteration.

So, for the next item in the collection (which was the item 3), the first argument provided to the + function would've been the earlier value 3, while the second argument would have been the collection item 3. That iteration would have returned the resulting value of 6 (i.e., 3 + 3 = 6), which would have then been passed as the "accumulated" value for the next iteration.

Now, on the final iteration we have the accumulated value 6 and the collection item 4, meaning the last execution would be (+ 6 4), which results in the value 10.

Let's see a more *explicit* version of the reduce function (Listing 3-11).

Listing 3-11. Explicit Accumulator Example of the reduce Function

```
(reduce
  (fn [acc, element]
    (assoc acc (first element) (last element)))
  {}
  [[:a :b] [:c :d]])

;; {:c :d, :a :b}
```

In Listing 3-11 we change a few things, the first being we're using an anonymous function instead of a built-in function. The reason we've done this is to visually demonstrate how the accumulator is passed into the given function. The second thing we've changed is the initial value of the accumulator. We're not using the first item in the collection (which would've been [:a :b]), but rather an empty map data structure {}.

This is where we can see the real power of the reduce function. We're able to convert one data structure into a completely different data structure. We can see that our anonymous function associates the first and last element from the second argument [:a :b] into the map data structure (referenced by the first argument symbol acc).

The result of that first iteration is {:a :b}, and as that is the last expression that was evaluated, it is used as the accumulated value for the next iteration. This means that on the second iteration we associate the first and last element from the second argument [:c :d] into the map data structure {:a :b} (referenced by the first argument symbol acc). This results in the final value of {:c :d, :a :b}.

You can do anything you want within the function passed to reduce, but remember that the last expression (or the thing that is returned at the end of the function) is what will be used as the accumulator on the next iteration.

Filter

The filter function is useful for "filtering" out values from a collection that successfully pass a predicate check. Listing 3-12 demonstrates an example of how this function works.

Listing 3-12. Example of the filter Function

```
(filter even? (range 10))

;; (0 2 4 6 8)
```

In this example, we create a collection using the range function (i.e., (range 10)), which gives us a list that looks like (0 1 2 3 4 5 6 9 8 9).

Each element in that list is passed to the even? function, which as you can probably guess returns true if the element is an even number or false otherwise, leaving us with the resulting collection (0 2 4 6 8).

■ **Note**   This function returns a list, but if you wanted a vector returned instead you can swap out filter for filterv.

Comp

The comp function is a good example of one of the tenets of functional programming: composition. It highlights the language's ability to composite a pipeline of functionality by chaining together individual functions into a coherent whole.

In Listing 3-13, we can see this demonstrated by code that accepts a string and returns it both in reverse and changed into upper-case. This may seem like a silly example, and it is, but I like silly examples, as they can make comprehending specific behaviors much easier (as "practical" examples usually require a fair amount of additional setup and context rather than just getting to the core of what's actually needed).

Listing 3-13. Example of the comp Function

```
((comp clojure.string/upper-case (partial apply str) reverse) "hello")

;; "OLLEH"
```

In essence, the comp function accepts a number of functions as arguments and then itself returns a function. The returned function can then accept a variable number of arguments.

In the comp example provided, we have used a few new functions we've yet to learn about. The reason for this isn't because I wanted to show you those functions, but more because the main function we're demonstrating (i.e., comp) works by constructing a chain of function calls; we need functions to feed to it.

At a high level, comp gives us a more concise way of executing the following code (Listing 3-14), which functionally works the same as the code in Listing 3-13.

Listing 3-14. Longform Version of the comp Function

```
(clojure.string/upper-case
  (apply str
    (reverse "hello")))
```

So, using the longform version, let's break down what the code does. First, we're reversing our string: (reverse "hello"). The result, a collection with each character in the string placed in reverse order—(\o \l \l \e \h)—is then passed to the apply str combination.

We've used apply here as we want to effectively splat each element within the collection into the argument list of the str function. If we just passed str the result of (reverse "hello"), it wouldn't have been able to convert the list into a string, so we're passing each string character within the collection to str instead (via the apply function).

■ **Note**   An alternative app roach to using 'apply' would be 'clojure.string/join'.

This will result in "olleh" being passed into the clojure.string/upper-case function (we saw this used in Listing 3-13), which then upper-cases the entire string to return the final result of "OLLEH".

Let's now quickly revisit our original solution, which used comp to solve this problem, and start to break down the differences. See Listing 3-15.

Listing 3-15. Example of the comp Function

```
((comp clojure.string/upper-case (partial apply str) reverse) "hello")

;; "OLLEH"
```

Although this looks complicated, effectively we have the structure (... "hello"), where the string "hello" is being passed as an argument to the function that comp generates (...) by compositing all the functions we provided it.

You should notice that the execution order for comp is right-to-left (much how Lisp syntax works: "inside-out"). So, although reverse is the last function specified, it's actually the first one executed. Then, the result of that is passed to the next function, and so on, until each function to the left has been executed.

One thing different in the comp example compared to the non-comp version is that we're using (partial apply str) instead of (apply str). This is important (and required), because if we didn't do this there would be an error raised, as Clojure would think we were trying to execute (apply str) without any arguments. So, we use partial to *generate* a function that we can provide to comp, and yet it will still execute as expected when the overall expression is run.

Another thing worth pointing out is that this isn't actually more *concise* than the longform version I demonstrated earlier, and by that I mean we could compress the longform version into one line and it would still be more concise than the comp version AND we wouldn't need to use the partial function to achieve the trickery we just looked at.

So, this begs the question: what's the point of the comp function, and when exactly should we be using it?

Well, if the number of functions for your pipeline is quite short (as in our example, where we're only using three functions), then you could get away with putting the code into a user-defined function (good for reusability). See Listing 3-16.

Listing 3-16. Store Longform Version Within a Function for Reuse

```
(defn reverse-and-upcase [s]
  (clojure.string/upper-case (apply str (reverse s))))

(reverse-and-upcase "hello")
```

But consider the example in Listing 3-17, where we're using the map function over a vector data structure and are converting each element within the collection into a keyword.

Listing 3-17. Convert Item into a Keyword

```
(map (comp keyword str) [1 2])

;; (:1 :2)
```

As you can see, we first need to convert the element (which is a number) into a string using str before we can convert that string into a keyword using the keyword function, and because map expects a function as its first argument, we're using comp to return a composite function that fulfills the behavior we require. This is a nice, clean, and elegant solution, a perfect way for the comp function to be used.

Now, compare that to the alternative solution (i.e., *not* using comp), seen in Listing 3-18.

Listing 3-18. Convert Item into a Keyword Without comp

```
(map #(keyword (str %1)) [1 2])

;; (:1 :2)
```

The map function expects a function to map over the provided collection, and so we need to provide an anonymous function #(...), and within it we call str while passing it the element from the collection (which is implicitly stored inside %1), and the result of that function is then passed to the keyword function.

I personally find this alternative solution *less* elegant. Although it's still pretty nice compared to other programming languages, it's more verbose and difficult to read than the comp version.

■ **Note**   A good article that breaks down a problem using higher-order functions (and demonstrates the alternative—a much less elegant solution) can be found here: `http://christophermaier.name/`.[3]

Partial Application

In the previous section, we used the partial function to demonstrate how Clojure can facilitate higher-order functions. But the partial function itself also demonstrates another important functional concept known as *partial application,* which states that you can gain more reusability from your code by defining new functions that are composed from existing functions with part of their arguments prefilled.

Partial application helps to promote the creation of functions that can expand their use cases beyond their initial intent. An example could be that you're creating an API for users to consume. Part of your API is required to talk to some back-end system that requires lots of parameters to be provided as part of the call (half of them are generic details that never change).

Rather than rely on the consumer of your API to provide all the values, you could expose a function in your API that is an already partially applied function. In your code, you use partial application to prefill certain params, and then the API consumer can fill in the rest (unaware there are extra params already set for them).

■ **Note**   See Listing 3-3 for a simple example of the partial function.

---

[3]`http://christophermaier.name/blog/2011/07/07/writing-elegant-clojure-code-using-higher-order-functions`

The concept of partial application is regularly confused with another functional concept known as *currying* (which Clojure doesn't support). When you "curry" a function, the function's arguments are expanded internally into separate functions.

If your function took three arguments, then, when curried, you would need to execute the function three times and provide an argument for each call (there's slightly more to it than that, but that's the basic concept you need to know to understand the difference).

A curried function won't execute its body until all arguments have been provided (similar to partial application). So, again, if your function accepted three arguments you could effectively call your curried function in one of the following ways. See Listing 3-19 for the first example.

■ **Note**   I'll be using a form C-like *syntax* simply to differentiate the principle of the example from actual Clojure code (which doesn't support currying). But be aware that there is no such native function available in JavaScript either.

Listing 3-19. Example of a Theoretical Curry Function with C-like Syntax

```
curried(1, 2, 3);
// all arguments provided at once in a single call

curried(1, 2)(3);
// two arguments provided, then a separate call for remaining argument

curried(1)(2)(3);
// one argument provided per call
```

Let's consider a slightly more fleshed out example (see Listing 3-20), continuing with the C-like syntax, but, again, this example is used simply to get across the principal idea behind currying so you can see how it's different from partial application.

Listing 3-20. Extension of Our Earlier, Theoretical Curry function

```
var fn  = function (a, b, c) { return a + b + c }
var foo = curry(fn)
foo('x')('y')('z') // 'xyz'

var bar = curry(fn)
var baz = bar('x')
baz('y')('z') // 'xyz'
```

When we look at the example in Listing 3-20, what we're in effect seeing is that internally the function assigned to the variable fn is being converted into a form that would look something like Listing 3-21.

Listing 3-21. Internal Representation of a Curry-Compiled Output

```
function f(a) {
    function (b) {
        function (c) {
            return a + b + c;
        }
    }
}
```

So, just to recap, the main differences between currying and partial application are as follows:

1. You only partially apply your values once. So, if your function takes three arguments and you partially apply two of them, then when your resulting function is called you only provide one argument. If you had instead partially applied only one argument, you would still only call the resulting function once (but this time you would have to provide the remaining two arguments).

2. If we consider the "API" scenario from earlier, *you* (as the creator of the API) are providing the initial values for the partially applied function, whereas with a curried function it is the *user* who provides the arguments.

Recursive Iteration

Programming languages that are mutable by default (e.g., JavaScript, Ruby, etc.) rely on the fact that they create side effects (and can mutate state) in order to execute their looping constructs.

The classic for loop you're likely familiar with, for (i = 0; i < 10; i++) {}, by design allows mutating local variables to increment the loop. In Clojure, local variables are immutable, and so for us to loop we need to use recursive function calls instead.

Instead of looping, you'll typically need to use the loop/recur special form (which we'll demonstrate shortly), although a lot of the time other iterator-style functions such as map, reduce, and filter will be better fitted to solving the problem at hand.

The main benefit of the loop/recur special form is that it allows you to safely apply recursive function calls without exhausting your memory stack. For example, if you've ever written any JavaScript code in your life you'll likely have hit a problem at least once where you've exhausted the stack and caused a "stack overflow" error.

I won't delve too deep into the memory stack problem space, so I recommend you read a blog post I've previously written on the topic.[4] In that article, I explain what *recursion* means and how *tail call optimizations* work. It helps clarify why a language like Clojure needs a mechanism such as loop/recur, as well as the purpose of a trampoline function, both of which I'll be demonstrating next.

---

[4]http://www.integralist.co.uk/posts/js-recursion.html

To begin, let's understand how the loop/recur form works. By using this form we're able to execute some code recursively. We start by defining where our "loop" begins (using the loop function), then later on in our code we'll need to define where the recursion should happen (using the recur function). If recur doesn't find a loop, it'll search for the next function in order for it to restart from that. The example in Listing 3-22 gives a simple example of its use.

Listing 3-22. Example of a Simple loop/recur

```
(loop [i 10]
  (if (= i 0)
    (prn "finished")
    (recur (do (prn i) (dec i)))))
```

The output of Listing 3-22 should be the numbers 10–1 printing to the screen in descending order and finishing with the statement "finished".

Let's break down Listing 3-22 to understand what's happening. First, we create our loop and bind the value 10 to the symbol i. This is our starting point. Within the loop, we have an if statement that uses the = function to check if i is equal to zero. If it is, then we know we're done, and so we print the message "finished" to stdout (i.e., the terminal screen). If the value isn't zero, then we call recur and pass it the result of (dec i), which decrements the current value of i by one.

This example demonstrates the essence of recursive function calls. We're not mutating local variables; we're instead calling the function (in this case loop) over and over but passing in an updated value/argument for each successive execution.

■ **Note**   You'll see we're also using a do function (do allows us to execute multiple code blocks). The reason for using it is so we can force the side effect of displaying the current value of i. In a real application, you'd probably just omit it, like so: (recur (dec i)).

With Clojure's recur implementation, you'll never exhaust the stack, and so you could change the value from 10 to 100000 and have no problems at all. A less-used function, but one very much related to recur and the problem of tail-call optimizations, is trampoline. The example in Listing 3-23 demonstrates how *not* using recur (*or* trampoline) can break your application.

Listing 3-23. Example of Stack Exhaustion

```
(defn count-down [x]
  (if (= x 0)
    (prn "finished")
    (count-down (do (prn x) (dec x)))))

(count-down 10)      ;; works exactly as previous example BUT it's not safe!
(count-down 100000) ;; will cause a "StackOverflowError"
```

So, in the preceding example (Listing 3-23), our function count-down calls itself (much like recur jumping back up to the opening loop). Each time that function calls itself, it passes an updated value for x. But unlike recur, which protects against the JVM's not providing tail-call optimizations, this implementation is doomed to fail if given a large value such as 100,000.

If we didn't want to use recur, we could still work around this issue by utilizing trampoline. I've already discussed the inner workings of how trampolining works in a blog post,[5] but in summary, rather than automatically calling the function over and over, the return value itself is a function, and trampoline flattens the calls for you so you don't fill up your memory stack.

Resolving the problem with our code will require a two-step process. First, modify the else statement so that instead of returning a function *call* to count-down you return a function. We achieve that in the modified version in Listing 3-24 by adding # before the call to count-down. Remember: #(...) is a shorthand syntax for an anonymous function.

The second step is to not call the count-down function directly, but to pass it to trampoline instead. The code snippet in Listing 3-24 demonstrates the required modifications.

Listing 3-24. Example of trampoline Function

```
(defn count-down [x]
  (if (= x 0)
    (prn "finished")
    #(count-down (do (prn x) (dec x)))))

(trampoline count-down 10)     ; works fine still
(trampoline count-down 100000) ; no longer triggers an error
```

Composability

The fundamental concept behind composability is to facilitate the passing of data through many different "filters" that manipulate the data so it's ready for its final destination. This is similar to how the Unix philosophy works; Unix utilizes pipes (|) for passing the result of one function into another. For example, the shell command ps aux | grep java takes the result of ps aux, which returns many lines of output, and passes it through to grep java, which filters it down to only the lines that include the word *java*.

Being able to create a pipeline like this, one built up from different isolated units of functionality, is very important within a functional language (we saw this demonstrated earlier with the comp function).

The main reason this is such a key aspect of functional programming is that your units of functionality should be generic enough to be reused within many different contexts, rather than being overly specific to one environment and ultimately not being reusable.

---

[5]http://www.integralist.co.uk/posts/js-recursion.html

I won't demonstrate composable code in this section, as I think it's safe to say by this point that we've already seen many examples of how Clojure allows for composability. We've seen this via the use of comp and partial, as well as other enumerable functions such as reduce, map, and filter, and there are so many more useful composable functions, all within the standard core library, just waiting to be explored.

Summary

This has been an important chapter with regards to both functional programming concepts as well as how they are reflected in the Clojure programming language.

Within this chapter we learned about the six main tenets of functional programming: immutability (persistent data structures), referential transparency (pure functions), first-class functions, partial application, recursive iteration, and composability.

In the next chapter, we will focus on the concept of sequences and how they are related to collections, as well as on an important topic known as the *sequence abstraction*.

CHAPTER 4

Sequences

In Clojure we have many types of collections: lists, vectors, maps, and sets. Each of these collections is also a *sequence*. Clojure provides an interface that is known as the *sequence abstraction*, and it is this abstraction that allows multiple types of built-in functions to work uniformly across these different collection types.

Before we get into the sequence abstraction, let's start with a task that is common when programming in Clojure, which is the need to loop over a collection in order to carry out some form of side effect. Consider the following example (Listing 4-1), where we loop over a list collection.

Listing 4-1. Example of Triggering Side-effect Only (No Modifications)

```
(doseq [element '(:a :b :c)]
  (prn (str (name element) "!")))

;; "a!"
;; "b!"
;; "c!"
;; nil
```

In Listing 4-1, we can see that we're looping over the collection '(:a :b :c) and that for each loop iteration the local variable (element) is updated to hold the current collection item. As part of the doseq "body" we convert the item (which is a keyword) into a string using the name function, and then we append "!" onto the end using str. Finally, we print the resulting value.

So, in this example we're not modifying the collection; we're only creating side effects, the side effect being we're printing a value to the screen. The actual *result* of executing doseq is a nil value.

Now, we could use Clojure's for function to loop over the sequence and achieve the same side effects but with a *different* end result. See Listing 4-2.

Listing 4-2. Example of for Loop

```
(for [element '(:a :b :c)]
  (prn (str (name element) "!")))

;; (nil nil nil)
```

© Mark McDonnell 2017
M. McDonnell, *Quick Clojure*, DOI 10.1007/978-1-4842-2952-1_4

In the preceding example, the code loops over the given collection with the intention of creating a new list based upon the result of each iteration. But because we've not returned anything from the body for each iteration, we end up with (nil nil nil) being returned.

So, the real difference between for and doseq is that the latter is solely for side effects (and subsequently returns nil); whereas the for form is actually what is known as a *list comprehension*. So, let's move on to the next section to better understand what that means.

List Comprehension

Using the previous example, you could be forgiven for thinking a for is a lot like the map function (which we saw in the previous chapter). The example in Listing 4-3 uses map and provides exactly the same side effect as well as returns the same overall result as the for version we've just been looking at.

Listing 4-3. Use of map to Mimic for Example

```
(map
  (fn [element]
    (prn (str (name element) "!")))
  '(:a :b :c))
```

Compared to the previous for example, it would seem that the for is easier to read than the map version, so the question becomes: Which is more appropriate to use, and when?

Well, technically the for function is what's known as a *list comprehension*, which is a way to create a list from existing lists and which should return a list or an iterator. The reason to choose the for form over a map (and vice versa) will depend on two things:

1. Are you creating a new sequence from an existing sequence, or are you looking to modify an existing collection?

2. Are you wanting to use multiple collections, or not?

In the first scenario, for allows the use of "modifiers" to help create a sequence that is *smaller* than the sequence it's looping over, whereas map will always return the same-sized sequence.

In the second scenario, if you're using multiple collections the for form will produce different results than those produced when map handles multiple collections (as demonstrated in Listing 4-4.

Listing 4-4. Example of List Comprehension Using for Form

```
(for [x [1 2]
      y [7 8]]
  (do
    (prn x y)
    (+ x y)))
```

If you run Listing 4-4 in your REPL, you should notice that we end up looping over the second collection y twice. We take the first element from the first collection x and then loop over collection y. After that has completed, we take the second element from the first collection x and start looping over the second collection y again.

Now, contrast this with how map handles multiple collections (Listing 4-5).

Listing 4-5. Difference of map with Multiple Collections

```
(map #(do
       (prn %1 %2)
       (+ %1 %2))
  [1 2]
  [7 8])
```

After running Listing 4-5 in your REPL, you should notice that map actually loops only a single collection, but for each iteration it combines elements from the first and second collections (almost like a zip). So, on the first iteration it passed 1 and 7 to the anonymous function. On the second iteration, it passed 2 and 8.

OK, so what else is so special about list comprehensions? Well, they provide "modifiers," which control when the body gets executed. There are three modifiers Clojure provides: :let, :while, and :when. We can see the last item (:when) being used in Listing 4-6.

Listing 4-6. Demonstration of :when Modifier

```
(for [x (range 5)
      :when (> (* x x) 3)]
  (* 2 x))

;; (4 6 8)
```

In Listing 4-6, we use the range function to create a sequence of numbers (0 1 2 3 4) and assign the current element to x for each iteration. Within the binding block, we specify the modifier we want to use (in this case, :when) followed by the test it will verify against.

In our test, we're saying the body should only be executed if the current element (when multiplied by itself) is greater than 3. The body's result is then placed in a new list that is returned. Hence, when using the for form, we're really "building a sequence, from a sequence."

Sequence Abstraction

Clojure promotes the idea of programming to abstractions. In order to fulfill the requirements of what is known as the *sequence abstraction*, Clojure has to wrap some of its own data structures so as to provide a unified and consistent interface. It also is able to do this for your own code (which we'll see an example of later).

What this facilitates is for certain functions to be able to work with, for example, a map data structure and yet treat it like it were a less complex collection type (like a vector, list, or set). There is a side effect to implementing this hidden interface though, which is that sometimes when you pass a vector into a built-in function, you'll (depending on the function) get a list data structure on the way out.

But, again, thanks to the sequence abstraction, Clojure is able to apply its functions across multiple different data structure types in a way that works a lot like a traditional "interface," as found in other OOP languages, where the benefit is in allowing different objects to depend on an abstraction rather than on a concrete implementation.

What this means in practice is that vectors, lists, sets, and maps all share this hidden interface known as the sequence abstraction. So, although not all of these data structures are implemented in the same way as a list, they can all take advantage of Clojure's collection/sequence functions as if they were of the same underlying implementation.

To understand how this interface works, we need to realize that each data type has been built (or wrapped) in such a way that it provides the following three functions:

- `first`: return first element in a collection

- `rest`: return all elements except the first

- `cons`: prepend element onto the collection

Clojure provides a sequence library that consists of many functions that can be utilised when dealing with data structures that support the sequence abstraction interface. All the functions found within Clojure's sequence library can be implemented with the help of these three functions. This brings us to the `seq` function, which helps a collection expose its elements and consequently extends the use of the sequence abstraction interface. Hence, a lot of the sequence library functions (for example, `map`) will internally call `seq` on the collection provided.

■ **Note**   For a full list of functions, see Clojure's Seq library.[1]

In the case of `map`, it'll ensure a data structure such as a map `{:a 1 :b 2}` will be converted into vectors within a list. For example, `(seq {:a 1 :b 2})` returns `([:b 2] [:a 1])`.

■ **Note**   It can be interesting to check the types returned when creating a data structure. For example, `(type (seq [:a :b :c]))` returns `clojure.lang.PersistentVector$ChunkedSeq`, whereas `(type (seq '(:a :b :c)))` returns `clojure.lang.PersistentList`. Because the list is implemented as a linked list, it's possible to iterate in segments, whereas that's not the case with a vector, which is implemented as a hash table, so it's actually utilizing a "chunked sequence."

---

[1]`https://clojure.org/reference/sequences`

Once the map data structure calls seq on the collection, the collection is in a structure that allows for the utilization of the sequence abstraction interface functions for carrying out a mapping of the data as expected.

If you pass a vector into a map function, then seq will again ensure the data structure is converted into a list so it can utilize the sequence abstraction interface. For example, (seq ["a" "b" "c"]) returns ("a" "b" "c").

Lazy Sequences

Now that we know about seq and the sequence abstraction, what exactly is a "lazy sequence"? Well, this is a sequence whose collection is computed in chunks, and the best way to understand it is by way of example.

Let's imagine we create a collection of 65 numerical elements. We pass this collection into the map function so we can both print and modify each item within the collection. The code for this might look something like what is shown in Listing 4-7.

Listing 4-7. Lazy Sequences Compute Their Values in Chunks

```
(def v (vec (range 1 65)))
(def m (map #(do (prn %1) (str %1 "!")) v))
(first m)
```

If you run Listing 4-7 in the REPL, you should see the output is the numbers 1 through 32 printed on individual lines followed by the return value "1!". This demonstrates that the full 65 items weren't computed when accessing the data assigned to m (i.e., (first m)). But why is that?

To help understand why the complete collection of 65 items were not computed, we first need to know that map returns a LazySeq as its type. OK, but why were only the first 32 items printed when dealing with this LazySeq? Well, this is because lazy sequences are realized in *chunks* of 32, and the reason for 32 specifically has to do with the efficiency of the underlying trie data structure the collection is implemented with.

If we were to type m into our REPL, this would force the complete sequence to be *fully* realized (i.e., computed), and so we would see the remaining elements in the collection printed out and subsequently modified. Lazy sequences are a performance win for us.

Let's now execute the code from Listing 4-8 in our REPL, and we'll again be able to confirm the chunked nature of a lazy sequence.

Listing 4-8. Lazy Sequence Chunked Output

```
(def v (vec (range 1 65)))
(def m (map #(do (prn %1) (str %1 "!")) v))
(first m) ;; prints 1-32, followed by "1!"
(nth m 10) ;; prints "11!"
```

Notice that in Listing 4-8 when you try to extract the tenth item in the collection (by using the nth function) it doesn't print the values 1 to 32 again, as it did when you executed (first m). This is because the first 32 items in the collection were already computed by executing (first m).

So, what happens if we now execute (nth m 33), which is an index just outside of the first 32-item chunk already computed? Well, we would see the *next* 32-item chunk computed, meaning the values 33 to 64 would be printed to the screen, followed by the return value "34!" (which is what was assigned to index 33).

As we saw earlier, if I request an index that is now already computed, such as (nth m 50), we'll not see any values from that specific 32-item grouping printed again. We'll only see the cached return value printed.

But don't go thinking you can now just create an unfeasibly large collection, such as executing (range 1 999999999), because the collection itself is still realized (i.e., placed in memory) upon creation. Executing that range in a REPL would cause you to stare at a blank screen while it computed each value.

There is a way to side-step that, which is to assign the computation to a variable so the item isn't computed until the variable is referenced. For example, the following snippet immediately returns focus when executed within the REPL environment: (def r (range 1 999999999)).

■ **Note**   A *large* range is of type LongRange whereas an *infinite* range, which you can create with (range), is of type Iterate and is an iterator that yields values (similar to a generator in other programming languages, like Python).

---

lazy-seq

This brings us to the function lazy-seq, which creates a type of sequence that doesn't "compute" any of the elements within the collection until they are requested (i.e., a lazy sequence). It's useful for allowing user-defined functions to also create these types of sequences, not just those sequence functions that are built into the Clojure language.

Let's see an example of how to use the lazy-seq function, and then we can begin to break down the moving parts and how it works.

Listing 4-9. Generate Your Own Lazy Sequence

```
(defn add-n [n, coll]
  (lazy-seq (cons
    (+ n (first coll))
    (add-n n (rest coll)))))

(type (add-n (range)))
;; clojure.lang.LazySeq

(take 10 (add-n (range)))
;; (5 6 7 8 9 10 11 12 13 14)
```

So, in Listing 4-9 we create a function called add-n. This function accepts a number (n) and a collection (coll). In the example, we've used (range), which creates an iterator that internally yields values as they're requested, but we could also have used LongRange (range 1 9999999999).

We can also see that the type returned by add-n is a LazySeq. Because of this, we know it internally utilizes the lazy-seq function. When we execute take on the lazy sequence we can see the result is a collection where each value of the given collection has had 5 added to it. So, a normal range call would result in a collection like (0 1 2 3 ...etc), whereas the resulting collection from add-n looks like (5 6 7 8...etc).

So, how is this working? Well, first we need to read (doc lazy-seq) and see what it has to say about how that function works:

clojure.core/lazy-seq ([& body])

Macro

Takes a body of expressions that returns an ISeq or nil, and yields a Seqable object that will invoke the body only the first time seq is called, and will cache the result and return it on all subsequent seq calls.

—Clojure documentation

OK, we can see that the lazy-seq is actually a macro and *not* a function. We also can see that it accepts a set of expressions, which it uses as its "body."

So, we know that our code is providing two expressions to be used as the body when calling lazy-seq. The first being (+ n (first coll)) and the second being (add-n n (rest coll)). Actually, you could argue it's more like one expression, as we wrap those two expressions in a (cons), but, ultimately, we're providing *some* number of expressions for the body.

The next thing we notice that is of interest is that our second expression is a recursive call to the add-n function itself. This is interesting, because you may then wonder how add-n wasn't causing a StackOverflow exception from endlessly calling itself (as there doesn't appear to be any logic defined to *stop* the function from calling itself).

Well, this is where the magic of lazy-seq comes in. It returns a lazy sequence, which in theory looks something like [<body>], where the body isn't executed until we try to access that first index. When we try to access the first index we will find the resulting sequence will look something like [<value>], where we no longer have a body of expressions to execute waiting inside, just the cached value. So, if we tried to access the same index again we would not actually re-execute the body, just return the cached value.

This explains why nearly all the lazy-seq examples you will see have nested lazy sequences (as our add-n function returns a lazy sequence and then calls itself recursively), because it's a good way to build up either a very large or infinitely sized sequence.

In our example, our "body" isn't actually executed until the take function requests the first index. From that index request we return another lazy sequence with a body waiting to be executed (remember *that* body will also return a nested lazy sequence with its own body waiting to be executed when called upon and so on forever, thanks to using an infinite range).

With this in mind, we can see that the take function is what effectively asks the lazy sequence to yield multiple values.

Let's consider a simpler example (see Listing 4-10).

Listing 4-10. Simple but Explicit Nested Lazy Sequence Example

```
(def ls
  (lazy-seq
    (do
      (prn "body executed")
      (lazy-seq (do (prn "next body executed") [:a :b :c])))))
```

We can see in Listing 4-10 that we have manually nested a lazy sequence inside of another lazy sequence, which itself has been assigned to the variable ls. Now, at this point nothing has executed. If we were to type ls into the REPL we would force the entire sequence to be realized, and so we would see the following output (Listing 4-11).

Listing 4-11. Output from Forcing Computation of All Nested Sequences

```
ls
;; "body executed"
;; "next body executed"
;; (:a :b :c)
```

But, instead, what if we took just the first item using take? Let's see what the output of that would be (Listing 4-12).

Listing 4-12. Request First Item from Set of Nested Lazy Sequences

```
(take 1 ls)
;; "body executed"
;; "next body executed"
;; (:a)
```

OK, so we can see that by asking for the first item we forced the first lazy-sequence body to execute, which subsequently caused the next lazy-sequence to be returned and executed, but from there we took the first item from the vector we returned from that nested lazy sequence.

If we were to now execute (take 1 ls) we would simply see the result (:a) and none of the side effects of printing values, as the bodies are no longer being computed; it's just the cached value being returned.

Summary

Sequence abstraction and dealing with lazy sequences can be difficult to grasp. I personally find the best way to understand these concepts is to experiment in the REPL with different examples. Try it yourself and see how you might be able to utilize the seq and lazy-seq functions (look online and in the documentation for examples that might help you see the potential in what these functions can do for future Clojure programs).

In the next chapter, we're going to sift through some useful concepts related to Clojure functions, such as pre-and-post conditions, as well as highlight various useful functions and utilities found within the core and string namespaces.

CHAPTER 5

Functions

The Clojure programming language is built on the foundation of functional programming, which itself suggests a language rich in functions.

If we were to look through the available Clojure namespaces and list of public functions/variables,[1] we would indeed find a wide range of functions and behaviors for our applications to utilize.

I'm going to start this chapter by rounding off a couple of items from Chapter 3 that make sense to discuss in more detail here. We'll follow on from there by investigating both the `clojure.core` and `clojure.string` namespaces and the selection of functions contained within them.

■ **Note** The `clojure.core` namespace is loaded by default for us when using the Leiningen REPL.

Just to be clear: I'm only highlighting a small subset of available functions that I personally find interesting (and only those that I don't cover elsewhere in this book). I highly recommend reviewing the API documentation, as there really is a wealth of information there waiting to be discovered.

Anonymous Function Shorthand

We've already seen the syntax structure for an anonymous function back in Chapter 2. In that chapter, we also saw that the syntax could be shortened like so: #(...). One thing we skipped over previously was the fact that from within the function body you could access the function's arguments using the syntax %1, %2, etc.

The snippet in Listing 5-1 demonstrates a basic example of this.

---

[1]https://clojure.github.io/clojure/api-index.html

Listing 5-1. Accessing Function Arguments Within Shorthand Syntax

```
(map #(+ (+ 2 %1) 2) [1 2 3])

;; (5 6 7)
```

We covered how the map function works back in Chapter 3. As a quick summary reminder, the map function provides us the ability to execute a given function against each item within a sequence/collection.

So, in the preceding example, our anonymous function is executed three times. First, given 1 as an argument; second, given 2 as an argument; and, lastly, given the value 3. The anonymous function then modifies the value it has been given and returns a modified version of the collection.

Pre and Post Conditions

One really powerful feature available in Clojure is the ability to execute code just *before* and just *after* the function body itself. This allows us, for example, to validate the function arguments as they come in as well as validate the result of the function is as expected.

The syntax structure looks like that shown in Listing 5-2.

Listing 5-2. Syntax Structure for Pre/Post Conditions

```
(defn <fn-name> [<args>]
    {:pre  [<fn1>, <fn2>, ...]
     :post [<fn1>, <fn2>, ...]}
    (<fn-body>))
```

As you can see, we provide a map data structure just before the function body that contains :pre and :post keys (both are optional). Each key is assigned a vector of functions that will be executed either directly before the function body or just after it, and they should return a Boolean true or false value.

■ **Note**   You can refer to the function parameters within the :pre and :post functions, as well as refer to the function body's result in the :post functions, by referencing % (as we'll see shortly).

For example, imagine we have a function that is supposed to add two numbers together; the code for this would look something like Listing 5-3.

Listing 5-3. Example of Pre/Post Conditions

```
(defn my-sum [f, g]
    {:pre  [(integer? f), (integer? g)]
     :post [(integer? %)]}
    (+ f g))
```

So, with this particular example function, if I were to execute (my-sum 2 2) I would see the expected return value of 4. But if I were to call the function with one argument as a String type (e.g., (my-sum "2" 2)), then I would see the output shown in Listing 5-4.

Listing 5-4. Exception from a Failing Pre/Post Condition

```
AssertionError Assert failed: (integer? f)  user/my-sum
(form-init611908878853766826.clj:1)
```

This exception is informing me that the function failed to execute because the pre-condition failed to pass one of the validation functions I defined (in this case, the first validation function was verifying whether f was indeed an integer).

Now, imagine someone comes along and modifies this code so that the return value is the message "Result: " followed by whatever the resulting value is. So, if we ran (my-sum 2 2), then their expectation is for the result to look like "Result: 4". See Listing 5-5.

Listing 5-5. Modified Pre/Post Condition Logic

```
(defn my-sum [f, g]
    {:pre  [(integer? f), (integer? g)]
     :post [(integer? %)]}
    (str "Result: " (+ f g)))
```

What would happen is that when the function was called, we would clearly see that the changes had broken the code because the REPL would be displaying the error message shown in Listing 5-6.

Listing 5-6. New Exception from Failed Pre/Post Condition

```
AssertionError Assert failed: (integer? %)  user/my-sum
(form-init611908878853766826.clj:1)
```

This error indicates that the post-condition validation function has failed. For that person to fix the issue, they could modify the :post condition to allow a String response instead, as in Listing 5-7.

Listing 5-7. Modified Pre/Post Condition Logic to Fix Post Error

```
(defn my-sum [f, g]
    {:pre  [(integer? f), (integer? g)]
     :post [(string? %)]}
    (str "Result: " (+ f g)))

;; "Result: 4"
```

Or by removing the `:post` condition altogether, as in Listing 5-8.

Listing 5-8. Modified Pre/Post Condition Logic to Fix Post Error

```
(defn my-sum [f, g]
    {:pre [(integer? f), (integer? g)]}
    (str "Result: " (+ f g)))

;; "Result: 4"
```

clojure.core

The `clojure.core` namespace contains functions and macros for dealing with all sorts of requirements. It is the foundational library of the Clojure language. In the following sections, we'll highlight some interesting items and hopefully will encourage you to explore the rest of the namespace to see what's there.

Map Construction

Let's imagine you have a list (or vector) of values that you wish to construct into a simple map data structure. We can achieve this in a manual sense by utilizing the `apply` function (see Listing 5-9).

Listing 5-9. Convert Vector into a Map Using `apply` and `assoc`

```
(apply assoc {} [:foo 1 :bar 2])

;; {:foo 1, :bar 2}
```

But there is already a function provided in the core library that reduces the boilerplate required, and it's called `array-map`. The way this function works is that it accepts a list of arguments that it can then manipulate into a map. See Listing 5-10.

Listing 5-10. Convert Arguments into a Map Using `array-map`

```
(array-map :foo 1 :bar 2)
```

But, you can also utilize the `apply` function (as we did when demonstrating the `assoc` approach) and provide it a list or vector, as in Listing 5-11.

Listing 5-11. Convert List/Vector into a Map Using `apply` and `array-map`

```
(apply array-map '(:foo 1 :bar 2))
(apply array-map [:foo 1 :bar 2])
```

Pipelining

There are times when you need to mutate a let binding value but are unable to because let doesn't create *mutable* local variables. Here's an example to demonstrate the problem (Listing 5-12).

Listing 5-12. Example of let's Immutable Binding Value

```
(let [foo 1]
  (inc foo)
  (println foo))

;; 1
;; nil
```

In Listing 5-12, we wanted to increment foo, but by the time we reached the next form (i.e., println) we could see that foo had not actually changed and was still the same value as before.

We can solve this by using the as-> macro (Listing 5-13).

Listing 5-13. Using as-> Macro to Avoid Immutable Bindings

```
(as-> 1 foo
  (inc foo)
  (println foo))

;; 2
;; nil
```

What this macro does is bind the value 1 to the name foo, and then for each listed form it will rebind the name to the updated value. What's interesting about this macro is that you can use it for facilitating finer control when manipulating data within a pipeline. I'll demonstrate this in the following example using a threaded macro (Listing 5-14).

Listing 5-14. Using as-> Macro for Granular Pipeline Processing

```
(-> [9 8 7]
  (as-> coll
    (map - coll [3 2 1])
    (apply str coll)
    (str coll " is the number of the beast!"))
  (clojure.string/upper-case))

;; "666 IS THE NUMBER OF THE BEAST!"
```

In Listing 5-14, the thread-first macro is being used to pass [9 8 7] as the first argument to as-> (i.e., [9 8 7] is inserted *before* the coll argument). We then have a single form inside of as-> that manipulates the data using the map and - functions.

■ **Note**   For more info on - and how it works, please refer to (doc -).

The result from the - function is [6 6 6], whereupon we convert it into a string so it becomes 666. If we didn't convert it into a string first, then the end result would have been a little different (Listing 5-15).

Listing 5-15. Demonstrating Output When Printing a Vector Via str

```
"clojure.lang.LazySeq@8ba5 is the number of the beast"
```

Finally, we concatenate both strings together and then uppercase the last form result, which gives us back the result we expected. This pipeline would be difficult to achieve with a thread-first macro by itself, as the order of the arguments changes throughout the pipeline. To demonstrate that issue, consider the example in Listing 5-16.

Listing 5-16. Demonstrate Problem with Just Using thread-first Macro

```
(-> [9 8 7]
  (map - [3 2 1])
  (apply str)
  (str " is the number of the beast!")
  (clojure.string/upper-case))
```

There are two issues here, both revolving around the order of the arguments' being incorrect:

1. (map - [3 2 1]) needs [9 8 7] to be placed in front of -, not *behind* it, as would be the case here due to the -> macro.

2. (apply str) needs the result of the previous form to be placed *after* str and not before it, as would be the case here.

We could try to mix together the thread-first macro (->) and the thread-last macro (->>), like in Listing 5-17.

Listing 5-17. Utilize Both thread-first and thread-last Macros

```
(-> [9 8 7]
  (map - [3 2 1])
  (->> (apply str))
  (str " is the number of the beast!")
  (clojure.string/upper-case))
```

The code in Listing 5-17 would *almost* work, with the exception that the first form has a complicated requirement, which is that the placement of [9 8 7] needs to be right in the *middle* of the form. So, neither the front nor the back (as per the -> or ->> macros) will suffice, as we'll end up with either an error or a different result altogether.

Hence, using as-> as a way to allow for more-flexible manipulation is the appropriate option for us to use in this example. Now, if we look back at our original solution (Listing 5-14), we might think to mix that with a thread-last macro, like in Listing 5-18.

Listing 5-18. Mix ->> thread-last Macro with as->

```
(-> [9 8 7]
  (as-> coll
    (map - coll [3 2 1]))
  (->> (apply str))
  (str " is the number of the beast!")
  (clojure.string/upper-case))
```

But now we're mixing three separate types of pipeline functions (->, ->>, and as->), which makes the code harder to reason about, and with no real benefit either. The example in Listing 5-18 merely serves the purpose of demonstrating that using all three macros is possible. I personally would stick with the original solution of just -> and as->.

■ **Note**   If the pipeline work I was doing in real life were as simple as the example use, then in reality I wouldn't even bother with ->. I'd just use as-> by itself. So, excuse the example provided, but hopefully it has demonstrated the potential power of as->.

Dropping Values

Back in Chapter 2, when describing data structures, we took a look at the peek function, which would return the last item in a vector. There is a related set of functions you might find useful when you want everything *except* the last item from a collection.

For example, imagine you have a vector such as [1 2 3], and from this you want a collection returned that consists of just the first two items. You could achieve this in one of two ways. See Listing 5-19 for both.

Listing 5-19. Return Collection Minus the Last Item

```
(drop-last [1 2 3])
;; (1 2)
(butlast [1 2 3])
;; (1 2)
```

The difference between the drop-last and butlast functions becomes apparent once you read the documentation for both (see Listing 5-20).

Listing 5-20. Documentation for drop-last and butlast Functions

```
user=> (doc drop-last)
-------------------------
clojure.core/drop-last
([s] [n s])
  Return a lazy sequence of all but the last n (default 1) items in coll

user=> (doc butlast)
-------------------------
clojure.core/butlast
([coll])
  Return a seq of all but the last item in coll, in linear time
```

The butlast isn't as performant as drop-last, as it'll compute the collection values immediately (in linear time) as it isn't a lazy sequence that's returned. So, using drop-last is likely going to be more what you want to use the majority of the time.

■ **Note** There are also the rest and nthrest functions, if you're looking for everything but the *first* item.

Code Comments

Commenting out code in non-Lisp-based languages is easy. Typically, you'll stick something like // or # at the start of a line of code, and the code will be commented out (i.e., not executed).

Because of the structure of a Lisp program, this isn't as straightforward for Clojure developers. But one thing you can do is insert a comment function around your code to prevent code from being executed.

For example, imagine you had the code shown in Listing 5-21 that increments an atom value twice.

Listing 5-21. Increment an atom Value Twice

```
(let [x (atom 0)]
  (swap! x inc)
  (swap! x inc))

;; 2
```

To comment out one of the swap! calls, modify the code like in Listing 5-22.

Listing 5-22. Demonstrate comment Function

```
(let [x (atom 0)]
  (comment (swap! x inc))
  (swap! x inc))

;; 1
```

But be careful when using the comment function, as it will return nil, and that may or may not be what you want or expect. See Listing 5-23 for an example where the comment is the last form, and so the return value from the let block is no longer the result of swap (as it was in Listing 5-22).

Listing 5-23. The comment Function Returns nil

```
(let [x (atom 0)]
  (swap! x inc)
  (comment (swap! x inc)))

;; nil
```

Endless Cycle

Have you ever found you need to endlessly loop over a small collection of items? If so, then the cycle function is what you should use. The return value from cycle is an infinite lazy sequence, and so if you just called the cycle function by itself, then you would lock up your REPL.

In order to properly consume the cycle function, you will need to use the take function, as demonstrated in Listing 5-24.

Listing 5-24. Example of the cycle Function

```
(take 2 (cycle [1 2 3]))

;; (1 2)
```

So, what happens if we were to try and *take* one more item than what we can see as being available in the collection: [1 2 3] (e.g., take 4)? Well, in this example the collection will start to repeat itself. See Listing 5-25.

Listing 5-25. The cycle Function Should Repeat the Given Collection

```
(take 8 (cycle [1 2 3]))

;; (1 2 3 1 2 3 1 2)
```

Uniqueness

In Chapter 2, we saw how we could make a collection of unique values by using the set function to ensure any duplicate entries are removed (and placed into a set data structure).

The problem with set is that it *eagerly* creates the set from your provided collection, meaning that if you have a very large collection of items to pass into the set, then the full collection will be evaluated in memory.

Another way to remove duplicates in a more performant manner is to use the distinct function, which returns a lazy sequence. See Listing 5-26.

Listing 5-26. The distinct Function Is More Efficient Than set

```
(distinct [1 2 3 1 2 3 4])

;; (1 2 3 4)
```

As you can see, the distinct function works the same as set, in that it removes the duplicate items, but it does so by creating a *lazy* sequence. Because we're getting back a lazy sequence this time and not a set data structure, we have to realize there are different APIs for interacting with the resulting data structure as well as possible performance considerations with regards to Big O notation. Big O notation is used to indicate the number of operations involved when dealing with a particular data structure and how those number of operations change over time as your data structure gets larger (Big O is outside the scope of this book, but you can find more information online[2]). For example, you'll generally see $O(n)$ for a lazy sequence and $O(\log n)$ for a set.

There is also a dedupe function, which I feel isn't the best name for it as it can be a bit misleading. Dedupe will remove *consecutive* duplicates, not *all* duplicates. Listing 5-27 demonstrates its usage.

Listing 5-27. The dedupe Function Removes Consecutive Duplicates

```
(dedupe [1 1 1 2 3 3 1 1 2 2 2 3 3])

;; (1 2 3 1 2 3)
```

If you thought it would work like set or distinct and return (1 2 3), you would be wrong. As you can see, it's important to understand the difference between each of these functions as it'll help guide your use of each of them.

Predicate Functions

There's a small selection of predicate-related functions that I'd like to show you (remember that a *predicate* is a function that returns a Boolean true/false value). The functions I want to look at are as follows:

- every?
- every-pred

---

[2]http://www.integralist.co.uk/posts/bigo.html

- not-any?

- some

These are useful functions to know, because when working with data you'll often want to verify whether a selection of items match a condition completely or whether only some of them do (or even if just *any* of the values match the condition).

So, let's start with the every? function, which takes a predicate and a collection and will return a true Boolean value only if all the items in the provided collection themselves return true via the predicate (otherwise every? will return false). See Listing 5-28, for a demonstration of this behaviour.

Listing 5-28. Example of every? Function

```
(every? even? [2 4 6]) ;; true
(every? even? [1 4 6]) ;; false
```

What's interesting in the example in Listing 5-28 is that you can also use other data structures with every?, not just functions in the typical sense that you think of them. So, you could use a set data structure as the predicate and then every? would return true if every item in the collection also appeared within the set. Alternatively, you could use a map data structure as the predicate, and this would mean that each item in the collection would be checked to see if it appeared as a key in the map.

■ **Note** There is also not-every?, which is the reverse behavior. I personally find it so confusing to read that I'd argue that your code clarity would suffer because of it. I've also never had a need to use it either, as I rarely need to know if a collection of items *doesn't* match. Nevertheless, it's a tool at your disposal.

Functional programming is all about the composing of single-responsibility functions, and the every-pred function is a great example of the ability to easily compose logic checks. It accepts a list of predicate functions and will itself return a function. The returned function can then be applied against a list of items to see if they pass all the defined predicates. Again, a simple example will help clarify the usage (see Listing 5-29).

Listing 5-29. Example of every-pred Function

```
((every-pred number? odd?) 1 2 3) ;; false
((every-pred number? odd?) 1 3 5) ;; true
```

A moment ago I mentioned how the not-every? function was a bit confusing because that direction of checking conditional matches didn't make as much sense to me as the alternative, which is the every? function (as well as the fact that it feels more confusing—to me anyway—for readers of your code to use not-every? compared to every?). Now, there is a not-any? function that sits very much in that same camp for me. See Listing 5-30 for an example use case.

Listing 5-30. Example of not-any? Function

```
(not-any? odd? [2 4 6]) ;; true
(not-any? odd? [1 3 5]) ;; false
```

The reason I even make mention of not-any? (considering I'm clearly not a fan of the not-type functions) is because in an upcoming Clojure language version release (at the time of writing this will possibly be 1.9) there will be an any? function added to the core library, and that's something I'd recommend you take a look at once it becomes more widely available.

Lastly, we'll take a look at the some function, which every once in a blue moon you'll find a use for. The some function takes a predicate and a collection and will return true if at least one item in the provided collection passes the predicate check (otherwise some will return nil). See Listing 5-31 for an example.

Listing 5-31. Example of some Function

```
(some even? [1 3 5 7]) ;; nil
(some even? [1 2 3 4]) ;; true
```

OK, before moving on, it's worth clarifying that there is also a some? function, and I don't find it as useful as some alternative functions. What it does is return true if the provided argument is *not* nil. Now, this function is like the not- form of another function called nil?, which I find much more useful and easier to understand when sifting through code. The nil? function returns true if the provided argument is nil, otherwise it returns false.

■ **Note** There is also a false? function, which explicitly checks for the false value: (false? true) ;; false

---

Collection Extraction

There are some simple functions that can help reduce a bit of the boilerplate required in accessing the first item(s) within a collection.

The first function we'll look at is itself called first and works exactly how you might expect it to, in that you provide it a collection and it extracts the first item in that collection for you.

The other function we'll look at is called last, and it works, again, how you might expect it to, in that you provide it a collection and it extracts the last item in the collection. See Listing 5-32 for examples of both first and last.

Listing 5-32. Example of first and last Functions

```
(first [:a :b :c]) ;; :a
(last [:a :b :c]) ;; :c
```

> ■ **Note** The first and last functions return the *extracted* values, whereas the functions rest and pop *remove* the first/last value and return the mutated collection.

Now that we've seen how to extract the first item, let's see how we can take that idea further and extract the first item from the first nested collection using the ffirst function. See Listing 5-33 for an example.

Listing 5-33. Example of ffirst Function

```
(first [[1 2 3] :b :c])  ;; [1 2 3]
(ffirst [[1 2 3] :b :c]) ;; 1
```

We also have a fnext function, which locates the first item in the provided collection and then returns the next item along. Although, admittedly, that's quite a specific use case, and for most cases using the get function would be more flexible.

Let's consider two other functions: nnext and nfirst. The nnext function is interesting in that it locates the item next to the first item and then returns the remaining items in the collection, whereas the nfirst function extracts the first item in the collection and then returns the nested collection minus the first value. See Listing 5-34 for an example.

Listing 5-34. Example of nnext and nfirst Functions

```
(nnext [1 2 3 4 5 6]) ;; (3 4 5 6)
(nfirst [[1 2 3] 4 5 6]) ;; (2 3)
```

Ultimately, these are interesting functions to have available in the core library, but I do question how useful they are in the sense of code clarity. I know from past experience seeing these functions in someone else's code that having to look up the documentation made the flow of the code difficult to follow. But I guess if the right use case presents itself, then these could be a nice shortcut into the data structure you're dealing with.

String Formatting

String formatting is something I love having available in other languages and I feel like sometimes using str to concatenate different vars together isn't sufficiently eloquent. So, this is where a function such as format comes in. See Listing 5-35, which demonstrates how to interpolate multiple data types into a single string.

Listing 5-35. Example of format Function

```
(format "Hello %s, I hear you're %d years old"
  "Mark" 35)

;; "Hello Mark, I hear you're 35 years old"
```

In Listing 5-35, we can see we're defining a string that has two "placeholders." The first is %s (which indicates a *string* value), and the second is %d (which indicates a numerical value or digit). We then provide the values for those two placeholders as separate arguments.

■ **Note** Execute (javadoc java.util.Formatter) for full details of what formatting options you have available.

Frequency

When dealing with collections of items, you'll need to identify how many times a certain value appears in the collection. Thankfully, Clojure makes this super easy to figure out by providing the frequencies function. See Listing 5-36.

Listing 5-36. Example of frequencies Function

```
(frequencies [:a :a :b :c :c :d :e :c])

;; {:a 2, :b 1, :c 3, :d 1, :e 1}
```

In Listing 5-36, we can see from the output that we're getting a map data structure returned, where each of the unique values is made into a key, and the value assigned to that key is the number of times that unique value appeared in the provided collection. In this case, we can see that :a appeared twice while :c appeared three times.

Zipping Values

The behavior of interleaving different items across multiple collections is known in other languages as a zip function (much like how a zip on the front of a pair of trousers would interleave individual pins).

If you find yourself with two collections that you wish to "zip" together, then Clojure provides the interleave function, which accepts (at a minimum) two collections and then proceeds to combine each index together. See Listing 5-37 for an example.

Listing 5-37. Examples of interleave Function

```
(interleave [:a :b :c] [:x :y :z])

;; (:a :x :b :y :c :z)

(interleave [:a :x] [:b :y] [:c :z] [1 :d] [:e 2] [3 :f] [:g 4] [:h :i])

;; (:a :b :c 1 :e 3 :g :h :x :y :z :d 2 :f 4 :i)
```

You'll need to be careful using the interleave function, because if you don't provide an even number of collections, then the result isn't as obvious as you might think (see Listing 5-38 for an example of this).

■ **Note** I've spaced Listing 5-38 out a little so it's easier to see how the values are interleaved with each other.

Listing 5-38. Example of interleave with Odd Number of Collections

```
(interleave
  [:a :x]
  [:b :y]
  [:c :z]
  [ 1 :d]
  [:e  2]
  [ 3 :f]
  [:g  4])

;; (:a :b :c 1 :e 3 :g :x :y :z :d 2 :f 4)
```

In Listing 5-38 we can see that we have seven collections, meaning that once we reach the seventh collection, we need to pair :g with the next available collection, which is now the first collection [:a :x], as we haven't provided an even set of collections to interleave it with. So, because of the odd number of collections, we see :x is placed after :g.

Another issue occurs if you don't provide the same number of items in both collections. If that happens, then from that index onward (in both collections) the items are omitted (see Listing 5-39).

Listing 5-39. Examples of interleave Function with Odd Number of Items

```
(interleave [:a :b :c] [:x :y])

;; (:a :x :b :y)

(interleave [:a :b] [:x :y :z])

;; (:a :x :b :y)
```

So, we can see in Listing 5-39 that the second collection has no third item (:z) and so the resulting collection omits :c from the first collection. This helps to keep the resulting collection balanced. We can also see that this works the other way as well. In the second example, the second collection had more items than the first.

Clojure also provides a function called zipmap that allows you to map values with keys (much like interleave, including the potential to lose data) but returns a map data structure instead of a list. See Listing 5-40.

Listing 5-40. Example of zipmap Function

```
(zipmap [:a :b :c :d :e] [1 2 3 4 5])

;; {:a 1, :b 2, :c 3, :d 4, :e 5}
```

Interposing Values

The interpose function is similar to interleave in the sense that it interjects values together, but it does this in a different way. For interpose we only provide it a single collection, along with a string that indicates the value to be interposed. Listing 5-41 demonstrates how interpose works.

Listing 5-41. Example of interpose Function

```
(interpose " - " [:a :b :c])

;; (:a " - " :b " - " :c)
```

If you're looking to have the result be a single continuous string, then you'll be better off utilizing the join function from the clojure.string namespace, demonstrated in Listing 5-42.

Listing 5-42. Example of clojure.string/join Function

```
(clojure.string/join ", " [:a :b :c])

;; ":a, :b, :c"
```

Partitioning Data

The partition function is useful for dividing up a collection of items and not only controlling the size of the "chunks" they're split into, but also determining their "step" behavior and also how to handle the situation where a chunk doesn't have enough items to fulfill itself. Listing 5-43 demonstrates a basic example.

Listing 5-43. Example of partition Function

```
(partition 4 (range 20))

;; ((0 1 2 3) (4 5 6 7) (8 9 10 11) (12 13 14 15) (16 17 18 19))
```

Looking at Listing 5-43, we can see that we have a nice clean set of chunks created. But what happens if we were to change the value from 4 to 3? Listing 5-44 demonstrates this.

Listing 5-44. Example of partition Function with Changed Chunk size.

```
(partition 3 (range 20))

;; ((0 1 2) (3 4 5) (6 7 8) (9 10 11) (12 13 14) (15 16 17))
```

OK, so that was interesting. We've not been given a full set back. If you count the number of items, we have 18 and not 20. What's happened is that the partition function knows that it doesn't have enough items to fill the last chunk, which would have otherwise looked like (18 19).

You'll notice that we run out of items from our range by that point. The solution is to provide a "pad" (which is a collection), as shown in Listing 5-45.

■ **Note**   If we provide a "pad" then we also have to provide the "step," as it's the argument that comes second, so in the following example I just set the step to the default value of 1.

Listing 5-45. Example of Partition with a pad Argument

```
(partition 3 1 [:a] (range 2))

;; ((0 1 :a))
```

We can see in Listing 5-45 that we don't have enough items to fulfill the chunk requirement of 3, and so the third item in the chunk is the pad value :a. Similarly, if our chunk size was set to 4, then we could provide another value as part of the pad collection in order to provide that fallback value. See Listing 5-46.

Listing 5-46. Example of Partition with Multiple pad Values

```
(partition 4 1 [:a :b] (range 2))

;; ((0 1 :a :b))
```

It's also worth noting that there is a partition-by function that takes a function for deciding how to chunk the provided collection (see Listing 5-47).

Listing 5-47. Example of partition-by Function

```
(partition-by odd? [1 1 1 2 2 3 3])

;; ((1 1 1) (2 2) (3 3))
```

Simple Parallelization

The pmap function is *very* simple. It works exactly like the map function (we learned about the map function in Chapter 3), but it executes in parallel. This means that instead of passing each item within the collection into another function to be processed sequentially, multiple items in the collection can be processed at the same time.

If the function you're applying to each item in the collection is quite costly in performance, then you can really help to improve the performance by simply switching from map to pmap.

Consider the example in Listing 5-48, which demonstrates both map and pmap side-by-side and highlights how the API is the same. You should also take note of the time difference between the two (you should notice that pmap is much faster in comparison to map, simply because of the parallelization provided by pmap).

Listing 5-48. Example of pmap Performance vs. map

```
(defn slow [n]
  (Thread/sleep 1000)
  (println "finished sleeping")
  (inc n))

(map slow [1 2 3 4 5])
;; (2 3 4 5 6)
;; takes ~5 seconds

(pmap slow [1 2 3 4 5])
;; (2 3 4 5 6)
;; this should take a lot less time
```

If you want to handle some simple expression evaluation in parallel, then you might be interested in pvalues, which internally utilizes a Clojure *future* (something we'll read about more in a later chapter when discussing Clojure's concurrency features). See Listing 5-49.

Listing 5-49. Example of pvalues Function

```
(defn slow [n]
  (Thread/sleep (* n 1000))
  (println "finished sleeping for (* n 1000) seconds")
  (inc n))

(pvalues (slow 5) (slow 5))

;; (6 6)
```

When executing pvalues we can see that the return values from each of the individual slow functions are now grouped together within a single collection. But the key aspect of using pvalues is the performance gains, thanks to the parallelization it provides. When running this example in your REPL, you should see that, instead of the code taking ten seconds to complete, it should take half the time.

Repeating Yourself

Clojure provides a function that itself takes a function, and will repeatedly call that provided function over and over . . . *forever*. This function is called (can you guess?) repeatedly, and it can be useful for a number of use cases, such as simple data generation.

Because of the infinite lazy sequence that is returned, we need to utilize another function such as take in order to prevent locking up the REPL. See Listing 5-50.

Listing 5-50. Example of repeatedly Function

```
(take 5 (repeatedly #(rand-int 10)))

;; (7 4 9 7 0)
```

In Listing 5-50, we're using the rand-int function to generate a value for us (a number between zero and ten), then we call it over and over via the repeatedly function.

■ **Note** We use an anonymous function so that we can provide rand-int with an appropriate argument.

Finally, we use take to signify that we actually only want the first five items from the infinite lazy sequence that repeatedly would otherwise return.

Basic I/O

Clojure's core library provides two functions for handling simple disk input/output (i/o): slurp and spit. The slurp function reads in data whereas the spit function writes out data.

See Listing 5-51 for a demonstration that creates a new file and then reads it into the REPL multiple times. The first time we call spit we create the file initially. The second time, we use :append true to prevent recreating the file, and finally we call spit without append. We'll see the file is overwritten with the new content.

Listing 5-51. Examples of spit and slurp Functions

```
(spit "foo.txt" "abc") ;; returns nil, but creates foo.txt
(slurp "foo.txt") ;; "abc"

(spit "foo.txt" "xyz" :append true)
(slurp "foo.txt") ;; "abcxyz"

(spit "foo.txt" 123)
(slurp "foo.txt") ;; "123"
```

■ **Note** The `slurp` function also provides an `:encoding` param that defines what encoding to use when reading the file.

The `slurp` method is fine for reading a file if it can be contained simply within memory, but if we're dealing with a very large file then there are some other options available to us, such as Java's `BufferedReader`, which will allow us to read buffered lines as they're being read.

Listing 5-52 demonstrates how to use Java's BufferedReader alongside the `with-open` function to open a text file.

Listing 5-52. Example of `with-open` and Java's BufferedReader

```
(with-open [rdr (java.io.BufferedReader. (java.io.FileReader. "foo.txt"))]
  (let [seq (line-seq rdr)]
    (print seq)))
```

So, there are a few things happening in Listing 5-52 that we should be aware of. First thing we're doing is creating a Java FileReader instance, as that is a requirement for using a BufferedReader. The instance of `BufferedReader` is then assigned to the symbol `rdr`. From there, we can see that `rdr` is passed to the `with-open` macro, which acts like a context manager in that it will execute the body form internally within a `try/finally` form.

The "body" in our example is the `let` form that binds the symbol seq to individual file lines that are passed to it from the `BufferedReader`. We can see that we call `line-seq` and pass it the `rdr` instance, which it will convert into a lazy sequence.

The `with-open` function expects a list of items that it can call `.close` on from within the `finally` clause part of the try/finally form. In our example, it means we can be sure our `BufferedReader` will be closed upon completion.

clojure.string

The `clojure.string` namespace contains useful utilities for dealing with strings. As I've done with the `clojure.core` namespace, I'll cover a small subset of functions that I think are worth highlighting.

Checking for Whitespace

A common task is to verify if some input is actually blank. That is to say, is the input nil or empty, or does it contain nothing by whitespace characters?

Clojure already has an `empty?` function within the core namespace, but it only works with collections (not strings). If you need to verify this type of behavior with a string, then you need the `blank?` function (see Listing 5-53).

Listing 5-53. Examples Demonstrating the blank? Function

```
(clojure.string/blank? "") ;; true
(clojure.string/blank? "    ") ;; true
(clojure.string/blank? "    a") ;; false
(clojure.string/blank? "123") ;; false
```

■ **Note**   For the sake of simplicity I'm providing the fully qualified namespace path for the function. In practice, you'll likely refer in the blank? function from the clojure.string namespace so your code would look more like: (blank? ""). We'll see how to do this in a later chapter when we discuss namespaces in detail.

Beginnings and Endings

Another common task is the need to check whether a string starts and ends with a specific substring or character. For example, if dealing with a URL path you might want to check if the beginning of the string included a forward slash.

Clojure's string namespace provides two functions that let us verify this; they are the starts-with? and ends-with? functions. See Listing 5-54 for examples of both (notice though that they are case sensitive; we can side step this using regular expressions, but I'll come back to that shortly).

Listing 5-54. Example of the starts-with? and ends-with? Functions

```
(clojure.string/starts-with? "I am a string" "g") ;; false
(clojure.string/starts-with? "I am a string" "i") ;; false
(clojure.string/starts-with? "I am a string" "I") ;; true
(clojure.string/starts-with? "I am a string" "I am") ;; true

(clojure.string/ends-with? "I am a string" "!") ;; false
(clojure.string/ends-with? "I am a string" "G") ;; false
(clojure.string/ends-with? "I am a string" "g") ;; true
(clojure.string/ends-with? "I am a string" "string") ;; true
```

Now, as you would have noticed, the functions demonstrated are case sensitive, and sometimes that can be an issue. One possible way to side-step that issue is to use a regular expression to pattern-match against. The discussion of regular expressions is outside the scope of this book, but I recommend visiting http://www.regular-expressions.info/ if you're interested learning more about the syntax and available features.

For now, let's try one of the examples that failed from Listing 5-54, checking if the string starts with an I or i, and then verify this using Clojure's re-find function. In Listing 5-55, you'll see that we compile our regex pattern using the syntax #"...", where everything within the quotes is our pattern.

Listing 5-55. Example of the re-find function

```
(re-find #"(?i)^i" "I am a string")

;; "I"
```

> ■ **Note** Clojure provides quite a few regex-related functions within its core namespace. I recommend searching through the documentation to locate them[3] (they're typically named re-*).

In Listing 5-55 we can see the return value is the match itself. If we had used a regex pattern that *didn't* match anything in the string, then the return value would have been be nil, meaning you could pass re-find as a value to Clojure's nil? function and it would indicate if there was a match or not.

One other item worth noting is the use of (?i) within our regex pattern. Although the concept it represents is provided by all flavors of regex engines, in this case it's defining a "case-insensitive matching" flag, the actual syntax is syntax specific to Clojure. In other languages or regex engines you'll typically see delimiters such as / used to wrap the pattern (e.g., /my-pattern/), whereas with Clojure we use #"my-pattern".

The flags for the regex pattern are then typically placed outside of the delimiter like so: /my-pattern/i. In Clojure we provide the flags *inside* the delimiters and at the beginning of the pattern instead.

> ■ **Note** For more details on the inline flags *and* the various types of flags available, please refer to the Java documentation for its Pattern class[4] (specifically "Embedded Flag Expressions").

Trimming Whitespace

When dealing with user input, you most often will want to trim off any unnecessary whitespace around the input.

There are three functions we'll look at to help us. The first is triml, the second is trimr, and the last one is trim-newline. See Listing 5-56 for examples of their use.

Listing 5-56. Examples of triml, trimr, and trim-newline Functions

```
(clojure.string/triml "some space at the start")
;; "some space at the start"

(clojure.string/trimr "some space at the end")
;; "some space at the end"
```

---

[3]https://clojuredocs.org/search?q=re-
[4]http://docs.oracle.com/javase/tutorial/essential/regex/pattern.html

```
(clojure.string/trim-newline "a newline\n\r ")
;; "a newline"

(clojure.string/trim-newline "trim newline\n\rlast one only\n\r")
;; "trim newline\n\rlast one only"
```

Summary

In this chapter, we started off by learning about the anonymous function shorthand syntax as well as about how pre and post condition checks allow us to verify that the input/output of a function is what we expect them to be.

We then began reviewing some functions from the core Clojure namespace, including functionality such as map construction and pipelining as well as various predicate functions and nested collection extraction.

Finally, we took a quick glance at a few useful functions from the `string` namespace, revolving primarily around checking various whitespace conditions.

In the next chapter, we'll take a brief tour of Clojure's destructuring capabilities and how they allow us to write very succinct code when dealing with input and how to extract the information we need.

CHAPTER 6

Destructuring

In this chapter, we will be covering the concept of *destructuring* in Clojure.

Specifically, Clojure provides support for what is referred to as *abstract structural bindings* . . . hmm? Yeah, let's break that down a bit.

What this means, for humans, is that Clojure provides us the ability to extract data from a data structure without having to actually traverse the data structure itself. This concept is typically referred to as destructuring.

Although this is quite a short chapter, I would strongly recommend that you spend some time upon completing this section coding in the REPL and experimenting with the syntax we show you, as this will help to solidify your understanding of the concepts much more quickly.

To understand how destructuring works, we will begin with a simple example (Listing 6-1) and continue on through more complex variations that demonstrate the elegant and concise code that can be achieved by utilizing destructuring.

■ **Note**   Destructuring can be applied to `let` bindings, function parameter lists, and macros that expand into a `let` or function. But I will primarily be using the `let` form, as it's the easiest form for demonstrating examples within the REPL.

Listing 6-1. Simple Destructuring Example Using a Vector

```
(let [[x y] [:a :b]]
  (prn y x))

;; :b :a
```

Looking at Listing 6-1, we can see that we define our local variables using the `let` binding. When we do this, we'll also notice that we have to wrap our symbols (x and y) in a data structure that matches the incoming data structure.

If you remember, a `let` binding typically looks like (`let [x 1] (prn x)`), where x is assigned the value 1. Look again at Listing 6-1. The incoming data structure [:a :b] is a vector, and so the symbols x and y are placed inside of a vector to ensure the structures match. The values :a and :b are then assigned to x and y, ready for us to use.

© Mark McDonnell 2017
M. McDonnell, *Quick Clojure*, DOI 10.1007/978-1-4842-2952-1_6

Listing 6-2. Simple Destructuring Example Using a Map

```
(let [{a :a b :b} {:a "A" :b "B"}]
  (prn a b))

;; "A" "B"
```

Looking at Listing 6-2, we can see our example now utilizes a map data structure instead of a vector, like in Listing 6-1. Because of this, you should notice that the syntax inside of the let form is now a map to match the incoming data structure.

What's also different is that now that we're dealing with a map data structure, we need to assign specific map keys to our symbols a and b. In this case, we're extracting the :a key's value and assigning it to the symbol a, and similarly we're extracting the :b key's value and assigning it to the symbol b.

One nice feature Clojure provides is the ability to make our code clearer and more explicit by way of abstraction. Take a look at Listing 6-3, and you'll see an example of this in action.

Listing 6-3. Destructuring Example Using :keys Feature

```
(let [{:keys [a b]} {:a "A" :b "B"}]
  (prn a b))

;; "A" "B"
```

Looking back at Listing 6-3, we can see the structure is slightly different now. We have defined a :keys field and assigned it a vector of symbols [a b]. These symbols represent the keys of the same name from the incoming data structure and will hold their corresponding values.

Let's now extend this example further and demonstrate how you can access the _entire_ data structure, as well as the specific extracted data.

Listing 6-4. Destructuring Example Using :keys and :as Features

```
(let [{:keys [a c] :as complete} {:a "A" :b "B" :c "C" :d "D"}]
  (prn a c complete))

;; "A" "C" {:c "C", :b "B", :d "D", :a "A"}
```

OK, so, by looking at Listing 6-4 we can start to see that a more powerful set of features is being exposed to us. When this code is being compiled, Clojure recognizes the :as field is denoting that we want to store the entire incoming data structure in the symbol that follows.

This means the symbol complete is now a reference to the entire incoming data structure, while the symbols a and c are references only to the extracted keys of the same name. You'll notice we didn't have to extract all the keys, only the ones we were primarily interested in.

Another item worth reviewing when destructuring a data structure is the :or field, which provides us the facility to implement default values for any keys that are missing from the incoming data structure. Listing 6-5 demonstrates what this looks like.

Listing 6-5. Destructuring Example Using :or Feature

```
(def a-map {:a 1 :c 3})

(let [{:keys [a b c]
  :as original-data
  :or {a 11 b 22 c 33}} a-map]
  [a b c original-data])

;; [1 22 3 {:c 3, :a 1}]
```

You can see in Listing 6-5 that I've actually spread out the syntax over a few lines, and that I've also stored the incoming data structure off into a separate variable just for the sake of readability; otherwise, the example can start to become a little noisy.

What we can see is the similar items we've already looked at–the :keys and :as fields—but now with the addition of :or, which defines a map with default values set for all the keys we want to bind our symbols to.

For example, we can see that the incoming map data structure has no :b key, and so our b symbol, which will attempt to reference an otherwise missing key, will now reference the value provided by the b symbol specified in the :or map.

Additionally, we can use & followed by a symbol, which will indicate that we wish this symbol to hold a reference to all the remaining values as a list. In Listing 6-6, you can see that we specify the symbol z after the & character, and so we can see it holds the value (:c :d).

The use of & means we've been able to facilitate this let block becoming variadic (i.e., able to accept lots of additional items).

■ **Note**   & only works with the vector data structure.

Listing 6-6. Destructuring Example Using & for Variadic Behavior

```
(let [[x y & z] [:a :b :c :d]]
  (prn x y z))

;; :a :b (:c :d)
```

One final item we should investigate is how to handle the extraction of information from *nested* data structures. Let's demonstrate this using both a map and a vector. See Listing 6-7.

Listing 6-7. Nested Destructuring Examples

```
(let [[[a b][c d]] [[:a :b][:c :d]]]
  (prn a b c d))

;; :a :b :c :d

(let [{{:keys [foo baz]} :stuff} {:stuff {:foo "bar" :baz "qux"}}]
  (prn foo baz))

;; "bar" "qux"
```

Looking back at Listing 6-7, and starting with the first example, we can see that we're still effectively doing the same thing as before. We have an understanding of the nested nature of the incoming data structure, and so we're mimicking it when we attempt to destructure the data from it.

That means if we have a nested vector `[[:a :b][:c :d]]`, then we'll want to destructure it into a data structure that is also nested: `[[a b][c d]]`.

It's worth mentioning as well that the code in Listing 6-7 may appear to be quite difficult to read, but in practice your code will likely not look like this, as you'll be dealing with data that's coming from other areas of your application. This means you'll likely have variable references to the data, rather than inlined data (as we're using within the examples here).

For the second example in Listing 6-7, the nested map data structure, we can see we want to get to the data structure assigned to the `:stuff` key. So, in order to achieve that, we reference the `:stuff` key when destructuring, and from *that* we then destruct its values using the familiar `:keys` field.

■ **Note**   If your map data structure keys are symbols or strings rather than keywords, then you can use `:strs` and `:syms` in place of `:keys`, and this will work as expected.

At this point, all of our examples have been set up using the `let` binding form, but as mentioned at the start of this chapter, we can utilize destructuring with function arguments.

One interesting aspect of destructuring a function parameter list is that you can set up optional keyword arguments. Take a look at Listing 6-8 to understand how this works.

Listing 6-8. Optional Function Arguments Using Destructuring

```
(defn foo [a b & {:keys [c d]}]
  (println a b c d))

(foo "A" "B")
;; A B nil nil
```

```
(foo "A" "B" :c "C")
;; A B C nil

(foo "A" "B" :c "C" :d "D")
;; A B C D
```

We can see from Listing 6-8 that we've again used & to indicate a variadic function argument list, but now we're also using the :keys behavior to allow us to handle the extraction of map keys.

Summary

In this chapter, we've learned the important and useful concept of destructuring data structures. This can help to facilitate very concise and elegant code when dealing with complex collections.

We've seen examples of how to do basic destructuring of maps and vectors, as well as how to deal with nested equivalents and utilize the :keys, :as, and :or fields for further extending the available behaviors.

In the next chapter, we'll look at another useful concept known as *pattern matching*. What pattern matching provides is the ability to trigger *specific* functionality based upon predefined patterns. These patterns are applied to some form of input, and also (much like destructuring) provides some very nice and elegant code solutions.

CHAPTER 7

Pattern Matching

Pattern matching is the ability to trigger specific functionality based upon predefined patterns. These predefined patterns are applied to an incoming message (or user input).

There are somewhat related variations of this technique, which are referred to as *runtime polymorphism* and *dynamic dispatch*. In essence, these concepts refer to the selecting of an implementation based upon the known receiver at runtime. Pattern matching is similar, but from a practical standpoint is narrower in scope.

Clojure has a few different mechanisms for achieving this form of runtime dispatching of functionality. The first is to use a Clojure library called core.match,[1] and the other is to use a built-in feature called *multimethods*.

In the first section of this chapter, we'll look at core.match, and in the following section ("Polymorphism") we'll look at the multimethods implementation.

core.match

To use core.match, you'll need to tell Leiningen to load it, as it's not part of the standard core library built into Clojure.

The easiest way to do this right now—as we're still running all our examples within the REPL—is to stop the REPL you currently have open and to create a project.clj file (see Listing 7-1).

Listing 7-1. New project.clj File for Adding core.match Dependency

```
(defproject test "0.1.0-SNAPSHOT"
  :dependencies [[org.clojure/clojure "1.8.0"]
                            [org.clojure/core.match "0.3.0-alpha4"]])
```

Once this file has been created, start up the REPL again using lein repl; you should find that Leiningen will use the content of project.clj to set up its environment. Once the REPL has started, you can try executing the code shown in Listing 7-2 to pull in the match function.

---

[1] https://github.com/clojure/core.match

© Mark McDonnell 2017
M. McDonnell, *Quick Clojure*, DOI 10.1007/978-1-4842-2952-1_7

Listing 7-2. Load the `match` Function from the `core.match` Namespace

```
(require '[clojure.core.match :refer [match]])
```

■ **Note**   Don't worry about understanding the syntax of either the project file or the `require` function call, as I'll explain this when we start discussing Leiningen in more detail in a later chapter.

Example: FizzBuzz

OK, so at this point you'll have a `match` function available within the REPL, and we can start trying out some examples. Let's start with a simple example that comes straight from the `core.match` README (see Listing 7-3).

Listing 7-3. Pattern Matching Example from `core.match`

```
(doseq [n (range 1 21)]
  (println
    (match [(mod n 3) (mod n 5)]
      [0 0] "FizzBuzz"
      [0 _] "Fizz"
      [_ 0] "Buzz"
      :else n)))
```

What we can see in Listing 7-3 is the classic programming interview test: FizzBuzz. The idea is that you print a list of numbers starting from 1 to 20, but for multiples of three you should print the message "Fizz" instead of the number, and for multiples of five you should print the message "Buzz" instead of the number. Finally, for multiples of both three *and* five you should print the message "FizzBuzz." The output of the program should look like Listing 7-4.

Listing 7-4. Output from Earlier Pattern Matching Example

```
1
2
Fizz
4
Buzz
Fizz
7
8
Fizz
Buzz
11
```

```
Fizz
13
14
FizzBuzz
16
17
Fizz
19
Buzz
```

So, let's take a moment to understand what's happening in our code example from Listing 7-3. First, we create a collection of numbers from 1 to 20 using the range function, and then we print out the result of executing match against each item in the range.

The match syntax allows us to define some pattern types we want to match against; in this case, it's the result of (mod n 3) and (mod n 5), where n is the current range element (e.g., 1, then 2, then 3, and so on). If the current range number is a multiple of three or five, then mod should return zero.

What follows from there are the different expected pattern results and the functionality we want to trigger if those expectations match. In the example from Listing 7-3, we first check that, if the results of both mod functions are zero, then return "FizzBuzz": [0 0] "FizzBuzz". Otherwise, if that fails, we fall through to the next conditional pattern check.

The next expectation is checking whether we were able to evenly divide the range number by three: [0 _] "Fizz". You'll see we use the underscore character _ to act as a wildcard for the check for whether the range number was a multiple of five. We do this because we don't care what was returned for that check (because if the value was a multiple of five, then we would have already found a complete match in the first step).

If that expectation didn't match, then we would fall through to the next expectation: [_ 0]. This is the reverse of the previous check, where we now use _ when checking to see if the number was a multiple of three (as, again, we don't care what the value is). We then check if the other value *was* a multiple of five, then the result should come in as zero, and so a match should be found at that point and the word "Buzz" printed.

You can see at the end of our code we use the :else statement to catch and return the provided range number for when no match is found. This code provides all the requirements necessary for a successful FizzBuzz test.

Backreferences

You've already seen that we can provide the wildcard symbol _ to indicate that we don't care about the value. But we could instead provide a symbol to take the place of the incoming value. What this allows us to do is reuse the value inside the returned expression that is executed when a match is made.

This will be easier to understand with an example, so take a look at Listing 7-5, which demonstrates the concept we're describing. If you're familiar with how regular expressions work, you may notice that this behavior is similar to how you would use backreferences.[2]

Listing 7-5. Backreferences When Pattern Matching

```
(let [x 1 y 2 z 3]
  (match [x y z]
    [1 2 b] [:a0 b]
    [a 2 3] [:a1 a]))

;; [:a0 3]
```

In Listing 7-5, we have x, y, and z holding the values 1, 2, and 3 respectively. We pass these symbols through to match and define two sets of patterns we hope to match against ([1 2 b] and [a 2 3]).

You'll notice that the symbols b and a, which we've referenced inside of each pattern section, have not actually been defined anywhere. These symbols are handled internally by match, which assigns them the value that is incoming from the match argument list.

So, in this case, the symbol b will be assigned z (which we can see is the value 3), and the symbol a in the next pattern will be assigned x (which we can see is actually the value 1). We can use any valid symbol, but you would likely want to not use the same symbols already defined in the arguments.

Matching Literals

In the previous examples, we've been matching values based upon symbols. But we can also match on literal values (see Listing 7-6).

Listing 7-6. Pattern Matching with Literal Values

```
(match ['foobar]
  ['foobar] :bar
  ['bazqux] :qux)

;; :bar
```

In Listing 7-6, we're passing in a *literal* symbol to match against. In this case, the symbol doesn't point to any other value; it effectively evaluates to itself. We then have an associated pattern that matches directly with it, and so we have a successful match and return the appropriate value.

Now, if we also need to provide a fallback mechanism (such as when we fail to find a match), then we can use the :else keyword, as demonstrated in Listing 7-7. We saw this used earlier in the implementation for the FizzBuzz test, where if no match was found we

---

[2]http://www.regular-expressions.info/backref.html

would want to return neither "Fizz" nor "Buzz" nor "FizzBuzz", but just the incoming range number.

Listing 7-7. Provide Fallback Using :else Statement

```
(let [a (+ 1 1)]
  (match [99]
    [a]    :success
    :else :fail))

;; :fail
```

Matching Data Structures

At this point, we've seen matching against both expressions and direct literal values. But it's also possible to compare data structures.

Listing 7-8. Pattern Matching with Data Structures

```
(match [[:a :b :c]]
  [[:a :b _]] :success
  :else :fail)

;; :success

(match [{:a 1 :b 1}]
  [{:a _ :b 2}] :foo
  [{:a 1 :b _}] :bar
  :else :baz)

;; :bar
```

We can see from Listing 7-8, that we have two examples. In the first example, we're passing through a vector data structure, and in the second we're passing a map. In both cases, we're able to find a match easily by utilizing the _ wildcard symbol to catch certain values we either don't care about or are unsure of what their values will be.

■ **Note**   When using a map data structure, you can't use a wildcard on the key; it can only be used on the key's value.

When using a vector, you might only need a partial match. For example, you might only want to match against the first couple of items in the collection. If that's the case, you can use the & rest parameter (which you'll recognize from Chapter 6). See Listing 7-9 for an example.

Listing 7-9. Partial Pattern Matching with the Rest Symbol &

```
(match [[:a 1 :b 2 :c 3 :d 4]]
  [[:a 1 :b 2]] "this would need to be complete match"
  [[:a 1 :b _ & rest]] "rest allows for a partial match"
  :else :fail)

;; "rest allows for a partial match"
```

Safeguarding

Before moving on to looking at polymorphism, I want to demonstrate a few other features of core.match, such as how, when using a map data structure, you can end up with a partial match unintentionally, as well as how to use the :or modifier to implement safeguards for the data being validated.

Listing 7-10. Accidental Partial Pattern Match

```
(match [{:a 1 :b 2 :c 3 :d 4}]
  [{:a _ :b 2}] "maps default to partial matching"
  :else :fail)

;; "maps default to partial matching"
```

In Listing 7-10, we can see that unlike with vectors, where you can use the & rest symbol to implement an explicit partial match, the map data structure triggers a partial match as its default behavior.

You should be aware of this so that you don't accidentally match something you would rather avoid. It would be best in these situations to have a more explicit match defined in order to prevent accidental matching.

Alternatively, you can use the :only modifier to define which keys you will accept, and thus prevent an accidental match from occurring. See Listing 7-11, which demonstrates the implementation.

Listing 7-11. Use :only Modifier to Avoid Accidental Pattern Match

```
(match [{:a 1 :b 2 :c 3 :d 4}]
  [({:a _ :b 2} :only [:a :b :c])] "Didn't match, :only expects three keys"
  [({:a _ :b 2} :only [:a :b :c :d])] "Match!"
  [{:a _ :b 2}] "this assertion is never executed"
  :else :fail)

;; "Match!"
```

We can see from Listing 7-11 that we have an incoming data structure consisting of four keys (:a, :b, :c, and :d), and within our first match we're using the :only modifier to state that we'll accept a match if it only contains the keys we've specified. So, no match is made, and we fall through to the next pattern, where we again have potential for a partial match, but this time we accept it because of our modifier definition: [:a :b :c :d].

Now, in some cases we might want to have a variable number of possible matches within a single pattern. We can do this using the :or modifier. See Listing 7-12 for an example.

Listing 7-12. Use :or Modifier to Facilitate Variable Matches per Pattern

```
(match [[1 2 3]]
  [[1 (:or 3 4) 3]] :foo
  [[1 (:or 2 3) 3]] :bar)

;; :bar

(match [{:a 3}]
  [{:a (:or 1 2)}] :foo
  [{:a (:or 3 4)}] :bar)

;; :bar
```

In Listing 7-12, we have two data structures: a vector and a map. With the vector example, we can see we're stating that we expect the data structure to consist of 1 followed by either 3 *or* 4, followed by 3. If that doesn't match, then we try to match a data structure consisting of 1 followed by either 2 *or* 3, followed by 3 (this is what actually matches).

The map data structure example is effectively the same principle, but we use the :or modifier to identify the key's value.

Finally, let's take a look at the :guard modifier. What this enables us to do is to specify a function that verifies the incoming value is valid (and what is meant by *valid* depends on the function used). See Listing 7-13, for an example of how you might use this modifier.

Listing 7-13. Use :guard Modifier to Facilitate Type/Value Validation

```
(defn div3? [n]
  "A function that returns true or false
  if the parameter can be evenly divided by three"
  (if (= (mod n 3) 0) true false))

(match [[2 3 4 5]]
  [[_ (a :guard even?) _ _]] (format "We matched first %d" a)
  [[_ (b :guard [odd? div3?]) _ _]] (format "We matched second %d" b))

;; "We matched second 3"
```

In Listing 7-13, we can see that we have two expected matches. In the first, we state that we don't care about any of the incoming values inside the vector data structure, except for the second item (which is the value 3). But, we do want to ensure that the value is an odd number and is divisible by three.

So, in the first pattern we tell :guard to use the even? function. Well, we know that the value 3 isn't an even number, so that match will fail. We move on to the next pattern, which specifies multiple functions to validate against (and so we place them inside of a vector). The first function to validate with is the odd? function, and this will pass, as 3 is an odd number. The second function to validate with is our own user-defined function div3?, which again passes, as 3 is indeed divisible by itself.

■ **Note**   According to the documentation, neither inline functions nor shorthand functions are *currently* supported.

Overall, you can see what a power feature pattern matching can be for a variety of different scenarios. Let's now take a look at polymorphism and see what that has to offer us.

Polymorphism

In most object-oriented programming languages, polymorphism is the ability to redefine the behavior of a method based upon the object it is currently residing with. This means you can have a Human class with the method speak, and when called it will return something a human would say (e.g., "Hello"); but you can also have a Dog class with the same method speak, and when called it'll return something more appropriate, such as "Woof!".

In a functional language, where classes and objects aren't as prevalent, polymorphism is hard to achieve because of a lack of types; or, to be more specific, functional languages tend to avoid creating new types for every programmatic situation where you would typically create a new type if using an OOP language.

Clojure works around the lack of types by supporting *runtime polymorphism* (also referred to as *dynamic dispatch*), the principal concept being: dispatch a value that matches a recognized polymorphic function, and that polymorphic function will handle the behavior for the given value.

There are a few ways Clojure handles this, but the one we're interested in is via the use of a feature known as *multimethods*. Let's take a look at a simple example of multimethods (see Listing 7-14) to understand how it achieves polymorphism within Clojure.

Listing 7-14. Example of Multimethod Functionality

```
(defmulti foo :some-key)

(defmethod foo :a [this] (str "foo :a given " this))
(defmethod foo :b [this] (str "foo :b given " this))
(defmethod foo :c [this] (str "foo :c given " this))

(foo {:some-key :a}) ;; "foo :a given {:some-key :a}"
(foo {:some-key :b}) ;; "foo :b given {:some-key :b}"
(foo {:some-key :c}) ;; "foo :c given {:some-key :c}"
```

We start by calling the macro defmulti, and we pass it a name (in this case, our name is the symbol foo). We also provide it a *dispatch function* (in our example, this would be the argument :some-key).

■ **Note**　You may remember that a keyword will act like a function when used on a map data structure.

At this point, we have defined a multimethod called foo, and we now need to define its *behavior* for each of the different types it might be associated with. That's where the defmethod macro comes in.

You can see when defining each defmethod that we make sure to give it the same name as defmulti (foo) along with a value we want to match upon (in this case, we define :a, :b, and :c for each variation of foo).

In the square brackets for each defmethod definition, you can see we pass in a symbol (in this case, this) that refers to the type the method is associated with. So, in our example, the value assigned to the symbol this would be {:some-key :a}, {:some-key :b}, or {:some-key :c}, depending on the variation of foo that finds a match when the call to foo is made.

■ **Note**　I've named the type this (in the spirit of OOP, whose self value is usually referred to as this), but you could have named it anything you like.

The body of each defmethod is what follows the square brackets, and this defines the behavior we want each version of defmethod to have. You would put whatever you need there. In our example, we're simply returning the relevant this value depending on the matched type.

This means, as you can see from the example in Listing 7-14, we can now call foo with a map data structure and have the appropriate downstream behavior triggered. For reference, the syntax structure is as shown in Listing 7-15.

Listing 7-15. Multimethod Syntax Structure

```
(defmulti
  polymorphic-function-name
  dispatch-function)

(defmethod
  polymorphic-function-name
  pattern-value-to-match
  [symbol-for-type]
  function-behaviour)

(polymorphic-function-name
  some-data)
```

Before moving on, let's review one other quick example for the purpose of demonstrating how the :default option works. We'll keep with the same example as before, but we'll extend it slightly (see Listing 7-16).

Listing 7-16. Demonstrating the :default Option

```
(defmulti foo :some-key)

(defmethod foo :a [this] (prn "A"))

(defmethod foo :default [this]
  (prn (str "Sorry, no idea what to do with '" (:some-key this) "' ?")))

(foo {:some-key :a}) ;; "A"
(foo {:some-key :d}) ;; "Sorry, no idea what to do with ':d' ?"
```

As you can see, we have defined a new foo type that will be matched by :default if no other match can be found. We've not defined a defmethod that expects the value :d, and so the :default will be matched as a fallback.

Summary

In this chapter, we've learned two sides of the concept of pattern matching, the first being pattern matching in the strict sense using core.match, and the second being via polymorphic methods and being able to use dynamic dispatch to trigger specific behavior. For both styles, we looked at the various syntax differences and how to safeguard our code against input that might not have any matching items.

In the next chapter, we'll look at a big topic: concurrency. There, we will cover a lot of different options for dealing with code in an asynchronous fashion, which can also help the performance and safety of our applications.

CHAPTER 8

■ ■ ■

Concurrency

One of the main selling points of Clojure as a functional language is its concurrency mechanisms (of which it has quite a few). In order to understand what concurrency means, we first need to understand the problem space it's related to and what it means for a program to run tasks concurrently.

A computer process (e.g., an instance of a program running on your computer) has the ability to spawn multiple "threads." Each thread has the ability to execute it's own unique set of tasks, and are separate from tasks executing within other threads. But threads spawned from the same process share the same memory space.

The fact that multiple threads spawned from the same parent process are able to access the same memory space can be a problem because if we're executing code concurrently (i.e., the CPU is "context switching" between threads of execution), then it means a change to a piece of data in memory can occur from multiple places.

This is why Clojure provides different mechanisms[1] for handling concurrency and to allow changes to occur in a synchronized and coordinated fashion. But when starting out with Clojure it can be quite difficult to understand why there are so many ways to handle immutable data in a concurrent fashion and, more important, *when* you should use them.

I've found the simplest solution is to use a matrix (Table 8-1).

Table 8-1. *Clojure Concurrency Types*

	Retriable	Coordinated	Asynchronous	Thread Safe
Delay			✓	
Future			✓	
Promise			✓	
Atom	✓			✓
Lock				✓
Agent			✓	✓
Transactions	✓	✓		✓
Channel				✓

---

[1]https://clojure.org/about/concurrent_programming

M. McDonnell, *Quick Clojure*, DOI 10.1007/978-1-4842-2952-1_8

> ■ **Note**   The "channel" type refers to (`chan`), which isn't part of the standard library and
> needs to be loaded from `core.async,` while "transactions" refers to many things (as we'll
> see later), one of which is the `ref` type.

In Table 8-1, you'll see we have four features: retriable, coordinated, asynchronous, and thread safe. Let's review what each of these means so we can better understand that matrix.

Retriable

For one of the listed types to be considered "retriable," a conflict must have occurred (e.g., multiple changes have been applied), and knowing how to handle the conflict must require retrying the operation.

One implementation for resolving a conflict is a CAS (compare-and-swap) operation, which is a low-level operation that's not directly exposed by the language API. A typical scenario would be when an attempt to update a value fails to apply because of a cross-thread conflict (e.g., two threads are updating a single value at the same time).

The "compare" part of a CAS operation begins by checking that nothing has changed. For example, it checks whether the current value has been tampered with by another thread. If that is the case, then the "swap" part of the operation is actioned and the requested update is applied. If, on the other hand, the CAS detects that a change has already occurred, then it'll get the *updated* value and retry the operation.

> ■ **Note**   The STM (which we'll cover later) is also considered retriable, and although it retries
> the operation it does not have anything to do with CAS per se (which is a low-level primitive).

Coordinated

For one of the listed types to be considered "coordinated," we would need to be utilizing Clojure's built-in STM (software transactional memory). The STM verifies the consistency of data across threads.

The difference between STM and CAS is that the STM will coordinate (i.e., check) multiple references, whereas CAS only concerns itself with its own reference.

The concept of a "reference" probably doesn't help distinguish CAS from STM right now, so, fear not, I'll discuss the STM in more detail later on when we look at creating and using the Ref type, and from there how the STM is considered "coordinated" and the CAS "uncoordinated" should become clearer.

Asynchronous

For one of the listed types to be considered "asynchronous," it should not block its current thread from processing. You might find that a particular type might not block because either it's genuinely "async" (i.e., it is running in another thread) or it's not a "blocking" call, but rather is simply waiting for its value to be resolved at some later time.

Thread Safe

For one of the listed types to be considered "thread safe," it must prevent conflicts when multiple threads are trying to mutate a shared value. We've already heard how this might be possible by using either a CAS or STM, but we'll see actual example code of this later on in this chapter.

Let's now take a look at some examples of each type so we can better understand when and how to use them.

Delay

The delay function is asynchronous in the sense that when you define its behavior, that behavior is not executed until some point in the future when you "dereference" it. Because of this, the delay function isn't a strict concurrent mechanism in the same way as, let's say, an atom or ref, and although people generally don't consider it part of the same family, it still has the ability to block your program, so I feel it's relevant for inclusion in this chapter.

To clarify, *dereference* means to acquire the value (and in the case of delay you're forcing some behavior to occur). You'll see all the concurrency mechanisms—agents, atoms, refs, etc.—use the function (deref ...) to acquire the contained value.

What confuses people is that dereferencing a value can sometimes cause your current thread to block, but this depends on the mechanism you're using, as well as on the context your code is running in. As we'll see later, an agent is non-blocking even when it's dereferenced.

If, on the other hand, the value is already available (i.e., it has been computed), then calling deref will return the value immediately. But if the value isn't ready, then maybe it's still being computed on another thread, and so your current thread making the dereference call will be blocked until the value is ready.

■ **Note**   A convenient shortcut for (deref x) is @x where x is a delay/promise/future/atom/agent/var/ref.

The delay function prevents an action from happening straight away. It is asynchronous until the point of being dereferenced, whereby it will block until the behavior has completed. Once a delay has been executed, it will cache its return value (see Listing 8-1 for example).

Listing 8-1. Example of Using delay

```
(def later (delay (prn "hello")))
;; returns immediately and doesn't block

;; ...some point later in your application...
@later ;; nil (prints "hello")
@later ;; nil (notice no "hello" is printed this time)
```

In Listing 8-1, we can see that the second dereference call on the `later` variable no longer prints the message "hello". This is because the action assigned to `delay` has already been computed and cached. In this case, there was no return value and so `nil` was returned.

When using a `delay`, you can also use the `force` function in place of either `deref` or `@` (see Listing 8-2 for an example). Clojurists tend to prefer `force` as it feels more semantically accurate (as you're *forcing* the delay to execute). So, pick whichever feels more natural to you. I personally use `@` so my code is consistent with the other mechanisms available that also use that symbol.

Listing 8-2. Example of Using `force`

```
(def d (delay (prn "hello")))
;; returns immediately and doesn't block

(force d)
;; nil (prints "hello")
```

■ **Note**   You can utilize a timeout mechanism with the `deref` function, but this only works when using a `future` or a `promise` (I'll demonstrate how the timeout works shortly). But be aware the timeout feature doesn't work with the `@` macro.

Promise

A `promise` is a lot like a `delay`, in that when it is created it won't block your current thread until it has been dereferenced. A `promise` is different than a `delay` in that it needs a value to be "delivered" first before it can be successfully dereferenced.

The benefit of a `promise` is that the value to be delivered doesn't have to exist at the point of creating the `promise`. The value could be the result of another function.

This is why a `promise` is useful as a "callback" feature; you can pass a promise around into other functions with the intention of dereferencing them while having a separate mechanism for the delivery of its value. See Listing 8-3.

Listing 8-3. Example of a `promise`

```
(def foo (promise))

(future
  (prn "child thread doing stuff...")
  (Thread/sleep 10000)
  (deliver foo :bar))

@foo
;; :bar (blocks until promise has a value delivered)
```

■ **Note**   A promise's value can't be changed once delivered. If you try to deliver a new value, it'll be ignored.

In Listing 8-3, we've created a `promise` and assigned it to the `foo` variable. We then use a `future` (which I'll discuss in more detail in the next section) to create a new thread and to deliver the value (in this case `:bar`) to the `promise` from that separate thread.

Finally, we dereference the `promise` within the parent thread and notice that the call blocks the parent thread until the `future`'s thread has finished processing and subsequently delivered the `promise`'s assigned value.

A `promise` is just a container that will hold a value. It is up to your application to decide when the `promise` actually receives a value, and it does this by passing a value using the `deliver` call.

Anywhere your code expects a value, you could use a `promise`. If you had a function that accepted a parameter, then you could pass in a `promise` and resolve it at some future point in time.

Future

A `future` allows the execution of code within another thread, which means it is non-blocking/asynchronous. If you wish to hand off a particular processing task to another thread, then a `future` is what you will want to use.

■ **Note**   Clojure handles the creation of threads from a thread pool and manages that internally for you.

At any point after a `future` is created, you have the ability to dereference it to find out its value. If the `future`'s thread has finished executing (i.e., finished computing a value), then calling `deref` will result in the computed value being returned.

Otherwise, if at the point of calling `deref` the future is *still* running, then the thread (likely the main/parent thread) that has attempted to dereference the future will be blocked until the value is made available.

In Listing 8-3 (see earlier) we created a child thread using a `future`, and within that child thread we purposely "slept" for ten seconds before returning a value in order to simulate a blocking I/O interaction.

The outcome of running the code in Listing 8-3 was that when the parent thread dereferenced the `future` it was forced to wait ten seconds before a value was returned (as the `future` hadn't finished computing the value when it was dereferenced by the main thread).

As mentioned earlier when discussing the `delay` function, you would more likely want to use `deref` over the shorthand @ macro in scenarios where you may expect a future to block, the reason being that the long-form `deref` allows you to specify a timeout as well as provide a value to fall back to if the timeout expires. See Listing 8-4.

Listing 8-4. Example of Setting Timeout and Fallback Values

```
(def f (future
        (Thread/sleep 10000)
        (println "done")
        100))

(deref f 500 "fail")
;; "fail" (blocked only until timeout of 500ms was reached)
```

In Listing 8-4, we can see that when we use defer we pass in a couple of additional args. The first is 500, which is the number of milliseconds we intend to wait for a response. The second is "fail", which will be the return value in case the 500ms threshold is exceeded.

It's important to realize that the task being executed in the separate thread will *continue* to be computed. The timeout is for dereferencing the value, not for the thread of execution. So, in our example, if we continued to wait and then executed (deref f) at a later time, we would see the value 100 computed successfully.

Atom

An atom is both thread safe and retriable. What this means is that an atom uses a technique called CAS (compare-and-swap) to ensure thread safety, consequently avoiding the complication of having to use locking mechanisms (which I'll discuss in the next section).

With CAS, if two threads are trying to mutate a shared variable then each thread will be allowed to make its change without being blocked by the other thread. The reason this works is because just before the CAS operation commits a change to the atom, it will verify that the value of the atom hasn't changed. If the value hasn't, then great—it'll commit the new value; but if the value *has* changed (e.g., maybe another thread got there first), then it'll restart the operation using the new atom value.

Updating the atom's value requires the use of a swap! function, which takes as arguments the name of the atom you want to mutate and a function that will be applied to the atom's value (see Listing 8-5).

Listing 8-5. Example of Using an Atom

```
(def counter (atom 0))
(swap! counter inc) ;; 1
```

■ **Note**   The ! suffix indicates a potentially unsafe method; unsafe in a functional language usually means it mutates state.

As you can see in Listing 8-5, we create a new atom, give it the initial value of zero, and assign it to the counter variable. We then use the swap! function to mutate the atom's current value.

So, in our case we used the inc function, but you could have used an anonymous function (or its shorthand variant) if you needed to mutate the value in a specific way or accept multiple arguments.

Listing 8-6. Example of Using an Atom with an Anonymous Function

```
(def counter (atom 0))
(swap! counter inc) ;; 1
(swap! counter #(+ 2 %)) ;; 3
(swap! counter #(+ 2 %1 %2) 3) ;; 6
```

In Listing 8-6, we increment the atom using the inc function. Next, we update the atom's value again using an anonymous function. Finally, we update the atom a third time using the same technique in order to demonstrate how the swap! function accepts multiple arguments that are then passed on to the specified function (i.e., our anonymous function).

■ **Note**   When using a user-defined function, be sure that it's idempotent (i.e., free of side effects), as the action could be retried and hence the side effect would be replayed as well.

In Listing 8-7, we utilize the set-validator! function in order to ensure the atom's newly computed value matches our expectations (if it doesn't, the value is discarded). In the given example, we wanted to ensure the updated value was always an even number. It's similar in spirit to a function's pre-post condition behavior, which we learned about back in Chapter 5.

Listing 8-7. Example of Validating an Atom

```
(def counter (atom 0))
(set-validator! counter #(even? %))

(swap! counter inc)
;; IllegalStateException
;; Invalid reference state clojure.lang.ARef.validate

(swap! counter #(+ 2 %))
;; 2

(swap! counter inc)
;; IllegalStateException
;; Invalid reference state  clojure.lang.ARef.validate

(swap! counter #(+ 2 %))
;; 4

(set-validator! counter nil)
(swap! counter inc)
;; 5
```

In Listing 8-7, you'll see that our validator function ensures the atom can only be set to an even number. If we try to use inc by itself, then it'll result in an odd number, and so an error is triggered and the change is prevented.

By resetting the validator function to nil for the specified atom, we effectively remove the validator from the atom. Looking back at Listing 8-7, you'll notice after we assign nil, setting an odd number (via the inc function) would be accepted successfully.

■ **Note** set-validator! also works for agents/vars/refs.

If you prefer, you can set the validator function inline with the creation of the atom by setting its :validator attribute (see Listing 8-8 for an example).

Listing 8-8. Example of Inline Validation

```
(def counter (atom 0 :validator #(even? %)))
```

Sometimes you might want to reset the value of the atom without worrying about the current value. To do this, you would need to use the reset! function: (reset! counter 0).

You might also want to change an atom's value only if its current value matches some pre-set condition. To do this, you would use the compare-and-set! function.

The compare-and-set! function works by returning true if the current atom value matches what you've specified (and subsequently it will proceed to apply the requested change); otherwise, if the current value isn't a match, then it'll return false and not apply the change. See Listing 8-9 for an example of how this works.

Listing 8-9. Example of Validating Specific Conditions

```
(def counter (atom 0))
(swap! counter #(+ 4 %))

@counter ;; 4
(compare-and-set! counter 4 0) ;; true

@counter ;; 0
(compare-and-set! counter 4 1) ;; false

@counter ;; 0
```

Notice in Listing 8-9 how the counter atom value stays set to zero after the second compare-and-set! function call. That is because we specified that the value be changed only if its current value were set to four, which it wasn't (it was changed before that to zero).

Finally, before moving on from atoms, we should also look at how to watch an atom for changes and to trigger some behavior once a specific condition is met. This is done using the add-watch function, which takes as parameters the name of the atom followed by an arbitrary name for the watcher and a function that will be executed when the atom is updated. See Listing 8-10.

Listing 8-10. Example of Watching an Atom for Changes

```
(def state (atom {}))

(defn state-change [key atom old new]
  (prn (format "key: %s, atom: %s, old val: %s, new val %s" key atom old new)))

(add-watch state :foo state-change)
(swap! state assoc :bar "baz")
```

In Listing 8-10, when we mutate the `state` map data structure (in this case, we associate into it via the `:bar` key, along with the associated value `"baz"`), we get a printout on the screen of what was changed. This happens because the change to the atom triggered the `add-watch` we created. The output of Listing 8-10 can be seen in Listing 8-11.

Listing 8-11. Output from Previous Program Using add-watch

```
"key: :foo, atom: clojure.lang.Atom@3e1b3567,
old val: {}, new val: {:bar \"baz\"}"
{:bar "baz"}
```

■ **Note**   To remove the watch, run (`remove-watch atom key`), replacing `atom` and `key` with appropriate values.

Lock

The use of locks is the classic first step taken to solve concurrency problems within a multi-threaded world. When you have multiple threads, all trying to access the same memory space, then conflicts will arise. A lock is a common low-level mechanism for handling concurrency, but is hard to use correctly. This is why Clojure provides higher-level abstractions in order to achieve "thread safety."

The way it works is by applying a lock around the data you want to manipulate, which prevents other threads from being able to manipulate the data while it is "locked." For example, if you have two threads running at the same time (A and B) and both want to modify the variable `foo`, then you'll find you have a non-deterministic event on your hands (i.e., you don't know if A or B will get to `foo` first).

By using a lock in your code, if it turned out thread B got to `foo` first, then by virtue of it getting there first it'll be able to apply a lock around `foo`, so when thread A tries to get access to `foo` it can't, and it has to wait until thread B is finished. When thread B is finished, the lock is relinquished so thread A can acquire it and prevent any other thread from accessing `foo` while it holds the lock.

Locks are not ideal, because they can be very complicated when trying to figure out the correct order in which to acquire a lock. The reason this is important is because locking mechanisms can cause what is commonly referred to as deadlock/livelock. This is more apparent within systems that utilize multiple locks (rather than simple examples that only use a single lock).

Deadlock

A deadlock is when two or more threads are trapped because they're waiting on the other thread to complete (but the other thread is also waiting for the other locked threads to complete), meaning no progress is made and the system locks up.

A common example given is of two people bowing to each other. The rules these two people have to follow are that you must remain bowed until the other person has the chance to return the bow. But if both participants bow at the same time, then they'll be forever waiting for the other person.

Livelock

A livelock is similar in ways to a deadlock, but is slightly different in that two or more threads can't progress, not because they're blocked, but because they're kept *busy* by each other.

The example typically given is of two people in a corridor constantly moving to the same side to avoid each other; they're not blocked, they're just kept busy forever trying to allow the other person to pass.

■ **Note**   An atom is different from a lock in that it uses CAS (compare-and-swap) rather than a lock mechanism; this means that a lock won't "retry" like an atom does.

Listing 8-12 demonstrates how to control access to a shared variable by way of an atom. In the example, we want to control how items are added to a vector. We want the result to be [1 2].

Now, before we look at Listing 8-12 we should clarify that atoms (as we've seen in the previous section) are already thread safe because they use a CAS mechanism to prevent multi-threaded changes' causing havoc, so there aren't many reasons to choose a very low-level locking mechanism over an abstraction such as CAS.

Listing 8-12. Example of Locking Blocks of Code

```
(def foo (atom []))

(future
  (locking foo
    (Thread/sleep 1000)
    (swap! foo #(conj % 1))))

(locking foo
  (swap! foo #(conj % 2)))

@foo
;; [1 2]
```

If we didn't utilize the locking mechanism around the swap! execution (you'll notice we have two locking blocks defined), then what would happen is an inconsistent execution path.

Imagine the locking blocks were not utilized in Listing 8-12. What would happen would be that the sleep called inside the future thread would mean that a call to swap! from outside of the future's thread would complete first, before the swap! from within the future's thread had finished computing, and so the result would have been [2 1] instead of what we were expecting, which was [1 2].

■ **Note**   In Listing 8-12 you'll notice we have to lock foo twice. Locking foo from within the child thread isn't enough to prevent the value from being swapped out. This is where things get complicated in real-world applications: in our silly example, the code for accessing foo is right next to each other, but in practice this is rarely the case, and so you could easily miss places where a lock should be applied, and consequently cause your application to break in unexpected and hard-to-debug ways.

Agent

An agent is a bit like an asynchronous version of an atom: it is a shared mutable value, non-blocking (until you attempt to dereference the value), and also uncoordinated.

■ **Note**   We've not discussed what *coordination* means yet, but we'll cover that in the next section. For now, it'll suffice to know that an uncoordinated type, such as an agent or atom, simply means a value that is independent.

In order to modify the value contained within an agent, you have two methods available:

1. send

2. send-off

Both functions have the same signature, (a f & args), which means it accepts a reference to an Atom (a) followed by a function that should mutate its value (f—this is often referred to as an *action*), followed by any number of arguments the action takes (& args). See Listing 8-13.

Listing 8-13. Example of Sending a Value to an Agent

```
(def a (agent 0))
(send a inc)

@a
;; 1
```

■ **Note**   You can fire multiple actions to an agent, and they'll be stored up in a queue and processed sequentially.

Now, there is a slight difference between send and send-off that you'll want to be aware of, which is that the former runs in a separate thread picked from a managed thread pool. The latter runs in a new thread specifically for the agent.

Most of the time you'll use the send function, but if you have an I/O blocking action you need to apply, then you'll want to use send-off instead, as this will allow that thread to take its time and ultimately not use up shared thread-pool resources.

One important difference between an agent and other types (such as atoms, futures, and promises) is that retrieving the value (dereferencing) for an agent doesn't cause the current thread to block. See Listing 8-14.

Listing 8-14. Dereferencing an Agent Is Non-blocking

```
(def a (agent 0))

(future
  (Thread/sleep 5000)
  (prn "increment the value")
  (send a inc))

@a ;; 0

;; 5 seconds later...

@a ;; 1
```

Because agents are completely non-blocking (even when dereferencing), if you need to ensure a group of actions have completed before continuing on, then you'll need to either manage this process yourself OR utilize the await and await-for functions that provide this behavior for you.

The difference between the two functions is that the latter allows you to specify a timeout: (await-for timeout agent). Let's see some examples that demonstrate how to use these functions.

Without wait/wait-for

In Listing 8-15, we can see that we send an agent two actions. Both actions sleep for ten seconds before modifying the agent's value. When we dereference the agent, it's non-blocking, and so we see the initial value (zero) is what's returned. If we dereference again later, then we'll see the final value.

Listing 8-15. Example of Standard Non-blocking Agent Dereferencing

```
(def a (agent 0))

(send a #(do (Thread/sleep 10000) (prn "added 5") (+ % 5)))
(send a #(do (Thread/sleep 10000) (prn "added 2") (+ % 2)))

@a ;; 0
```

Using wait

In Listing 8-16, we have the same example as in Listing 8-15, but this time we use the await function instead of a normal deref call. We can see that the returned value is nil, but we block until the actions are complete. Once it finishes, we can dereference the agent and get the final value immediately.

Listing 8-16. Example of Waiting for Actions to Complete

```
(def a (agent 0))

(send a #(do (Thread/sleep 10000) (prn "added 5") (+ % 5)))
(send a #(do (Thread/sleep 10000) (prn "added 2") (+ % 2)))

(await a)
;; nil
```

Using wait-for

In Listing 8-17, we have the same example as in Listing 8-16, but this time we use the await-for function instead of the await call. We can see that the returned value is false, which indicates that the timeout was reached and we didn't receive a value before the timeout was exceeded.

If we were to now dereference the agent, we would find the value is still zero. It will stay zero until the two actions complete. The benefit of using await-for means we're able to safely escape the blocking actions (which could be a very long time blocked).

Listing 8-17. Example of Waiting—with Timer—for Actions to Complete

```
(def a (agent 0))

(send a #(do (Thread/sleep 10000) (prn "added 5") (+ % 5)))
(send a #(do (Thread/sleep 10000) (prn "added 2") (+ % 2)))

(await-for 500 a)
;; false
```

Agent Errors

If you cause an agent to error, then it'll do so silently (depending on the error). In the past, I've caused an agent to fail and then later wondered why none of my actions (sent via a send call) were being actioned. Let's see an example of causing an agent to fail and how it reacts in Listing 8-18.

Listing 8-18. Example of Agent Failing

```
(def a (agent 0))

(send a #(/ % 0))
;; causes agent to go into failure mode (no error indicated)

a
;; #object[clojure.lang.Agent 0xf1c5585 {:status :failed, :val 0}]
```

■ **Note**   The last line of Listing 8-18 references the agent, and so we see the internal representation displayed. In that representation, you'll notice the :status :failed.

The problem with this silent change to a failed status is that all future send commands will also fail until the agent's status has been changed back to :ready.

If you need to verify what error an agent has received, then you can call the agent-error function and pass in the agent you wish to review; this will return the last known error for the specified agent.

At this point, there's a couple of things we can do: the first is to define an error handler for your agent so it becomes clear when an issue occurs, and the second is to restart the agent once your code is aware of an issue. See Listing 8-19.

Listing 8-19. Example of Agent Error Handling

```
(def a (agent 0))

(defn h [a e]
  (prn "Agent value: " @a)
  (prn "Agent error: " e))

(set-error-handler! a h)

(send a #(/ % 0)) ;; prints the following...

;; "Agent value: " 0
;; "Agent error: " #error{:cause "Divide by zero"...
```

> ■ **Note**   To remove the error handler, you'll need to call the `set-error-handler!` function again and pass `nil` as the handler value.

At this point, the agent is in a failure state, and so if you try to send another action to it, that action will fail to proceed. To resolve this, we need to restart the agent, and we can do that using (`restart-agent a 0`), where we provide the `restart-agent` function the agent (a) that we would like to modify along with the new value we want the agent to restart with (0).

If you would like to restart the agent with its last known value, then you could swap the provided value for the dereferenced value for the agent: (`restart-agent a @a`).

Now, you might want the agent to automatically restart itself. This is possible, but it's not as straightforward as you might think (e.g., just calling `restart-agent` from within the error handler). Listing 8-20 will demonstrate one possible solution that utilizes a future to decouple the call to `restart-agent` from the error handler.

The real cause of the problem is that the agent doesn't actually get marked as "failed" until the error handler has finished executing. This is why the use of a future fixes this issue, as it means the error handler can finish (as the future is executed asynchronously on a separate child thread) and the restarting of the agent will be successful.

I discovered this by wrapping the call to `restart-agent` in a try/catch statement, and this revealed the message "Agent does not need a restart."

> ■ **Note**   When restarting your agent, any actions that were queued up will continue to be processed unless you provide a `:clear-actions` true option when restarting the agent:
>
> `(restart-agent a @a :clear-actions true)`

Listing 8-20. Attempt to Automatically Restart a Failed Agent

```
(def a (agent 0))

(defn h [a e]
  (prn "Agent value: " @a)
  (prn "Agent error: " e)
  (future (restart-agent a 0)))

(set-error-handler! a h)

(send a inc)
a ;; 1

(send a #(/ % 0))
;; error handler h will be triggered

(send a inc)
a ;; 1
```

Transactions

Clojure comes packaged with its own STM (software transactional memory). In essence, the STM works a lot like a CAS (compare-and-swap) operation, which we saw earlier when looking at atoms. The difference between them is that rather than concern itself with a single value, like an atom (which is "uncoordinated"), the STM is able to refer to multiple values at once (hence, the STM is thought of as being "coordinated").

There are a couple of moving pieces when using the STM:

- dosync
- ref
- ref-set
- alter
- ensure
- commute

dosync/ref/alter

The first item (dosync) is the transaction container, and everything related to the execution of the STM should happen within that form. The second item (ref) is the "Reference" type that will hold the value to be stored/verified/updated.

All other listed items are functions that can only be used from *within* the transaction. This means any attempts to use the functions ref-set, alter, ensure, or commute from outside the dosync form will cause an error to occur. See Listing 8-21.

Listing 8-21. Simple Transaction

```
(def r (ref 0))

(dosync
  (alter r inc))
;; 1
```

In Listing 8-21, we create a new ref type r and assign it the initial value of 0. Once set, we open a transaction using dosync, and within that we pass the ref instance into the alter function, which applies the provided function (in this case, inc) to the value the ref currently holds.

Much like the atom type, we need to ensure that any actions that occur within the dosync block are idempotent, as the STM can end up restarting/replaying the entire transaction over again if a conflict arises between different references.

ref-set

In Listing 8-22, we'll use ref-set to change the value of the ref instance. This allows us to change the value using another direct value, as opposed to using a function to modify the value.

Listing 8-22. Example of ref-set's Allowing Literal Value to Be Assigned

```
(def r (ref 1))

(dosync
  (ref-set r 0))
;; 0
```

STM Restart Policy

In Listing 8-23, we will see the use of an alter function, again to modify the ref value. This is what you'll likely use most of the time when dealing with the STM. The STM will attempt to identify whether a change has happened to the ref outside of its transaction and will restart the transaction if a change has indeed occurred.

You'll see in Listing 8-23 that we attempt to modify the value three times simultaneously using multiple futures (remember a future will run in a separate thread to the parent thread).

Have a read over the code first, and then I'll start to break down the process taken by the STM in order to resolve the conflict that it is being presented with, thanks to a fairly simple multi-threaded program.

Listing 8-23. Example of How the STM Restart Policy Works

```
(def r (ref []))

(defn modify [r, f, a, s]
  (dosync
    (Thread/sleep s)
    (alter r f a)))

(future (modify r conj :a 2000))
(future (modify r conj :b 1000))
(future (modify r conj :c 0))

@r
;; [:c :b :a]
```

If you tried to dereference r immediately, then you would have noticed it only contained a single value [:c]; then one second later it would have contained [:c :b], and finally three seconds later it would hold the finished collection of [:c :b :a].

In Listing 8-23, we can see a user-defined function called modify, which simply starts up a transaction (using dosync), then sleeps for the specified number of seconds before using alter to modify the value inside the provided reference variable.

From there, we spin up three threads (using future) and execute the user-defined function modify within each thread while passing it the relevant reference value, function, and sleep arguments.

We've used very specific sleep values to demonstrate how in the application design process non-deterministic code doesn't necessarily complete in the sequential order it's defined in.

■ **Note**   Just to be clear, I'm only using (Thread/sleep) to *mimic* non-deterministic behavior. Your application code might use some form of blocking I/O instead that takes varying times to complete. Hence, executing that code multiple times can result in a different result order.

The process the STM takes in Listing 8-23 is as follows (this is an oversimplification, but it'll give you an idea at least of how it works):

- :a is passed (the code pauses for two seconds).
- :b is passed (the code pauses for one second).
- :c is passed.
  - The alter function causes the STM to check if the ref value has changed since the transaction started.
  - The value is still [ ] at this point (as the other calls are paused).
  - The updated value is applied.
- :b unpauses and checks the ref value (as it's about to apply the conj function).
  - The value is no longer [ ]; it's [:c], so the STM restarts the transaction.
  - :a is still paused by this point, and so the transaction completes.
- :a unpauses and checks the ref value.
  - The value is no longer [ ]; it's [:c :b], so the STM restarts the transaction.
  - The transaction completes, as there are no other transactions to cause a restart.
  - This means the ref value (eventually) is [:c :b :a].

In a real-world scenario, the time a transaction takes to complete won't be as clean as the example just used, but at least it gives you an idea of the process involved when dealing with the STM.

Nested Transactions

Clojure's STM implementation also supports nested transactions. In Listing 8-24, you will see two examples. The first will highlight how a nested transaction executed within a separate thread will start a *new* transaction, whereas the second example defines a new dosync block, but as it's running on the same thread as the outer dosync block, it doesn't create a new transaction and so the behavior/results are different.

Listing 8-24. Examples of Nested Transactions

```
(def r (ref 0))
(dosync
  (future (dosync (Thread/sleep 50) (println :foo) (alter r inc)))
  (println :bar)
  (alter r inc))

;; :bar
;; 1
;; :foo
;; :foo (indicates transaction restart, as ref was modified from outside)
;; 2

;; No new thread spawned, so ref is altered twice
;; While the inner transaction is not retried
(def r (ref 0))
(dosync
  (dosync (Thread/sleep 50) (println :foo) (alter r inc))
  (println :bar)
  (alter r inc))

;; :foo
;; :bar
;; 2
```

ensure

To avoid a dead- or livelock situation, whereby competing transactions are reliant on multiple references, we can utilize the ensure function to protect the reference from modification by other transactions.

In Listing 8-25, you can see that we have two references, current-account and savings-account, which when added together will result in a total value of 1100. The only condition we have is that the total for both accounts cannot be below 1000.

In the given example, we attempt to subtract the value 100 from both accounts simultaneously. Only one of these requests will succeed, as our constraint of needing 1000 as a minimum value means both requests can't succeed, because we'd fall below the constraint threshold. This dilemma is a good example of how a simple concurrency requirement can cause contention.

Listing 8-25. Example of ensure to Negotiate Multiple Conditions

```
(def current-account (ref 500))
(def savings-account (ref 600))

(defn withdraw [from available amount]
  (dosync
    (let [total (+ @from (ensure available))]
      (Thread/sleep 1000) ; allows for a more visible context switch
      (if (>= (- total amount) 1000)
        (alter from - amount)
        (println "Sorry, can't withdraw 100 from "
          (:name (meta (var current-account)))
          " due to constraint violation")))))

(println "Before: Current Account balance is" @current-account)
(println "Before: Savings Account balance is" @savings-account)
(println
  "Before: Total balance is"
  (+ @current-account @savings-account))

(future (withdraw current-account savings-account 100))
(future (withdraw savings-account current-account 100))

(Thread/sleep 2000)
;; sleep long enough to allow both transactions to complete

(println "After: Current Account balance is" @current-account)
(println "After: Savings Account balance is" @savings-account)
(println
  "After: Total balance is"
  (+ @current-account @savings-account))
```

The output you can expect from Listing 8-25 can be seen in Listing 8-26.

Listing 8-26. Output of Listing 8-25 Program

```
Before: Current Account balance is 500
Before: Savings Account balance is 600
Before: Total balance is 1100

Sorry, can't withdraw 100 from current-account
due to constraint violation

After: Current Account balance is 500
After: Savings Account balance is 500
After: Total balance is 1000
```

If we look at what's happening, it might look like there's a lot to take in, but remember that this is all code that we've already seen, and so by reading through it line by line you should be able to see that ultimately, we're using ensure to protect the type (in this case, available) from modification while within the transaction.

If available is modified outside the transaction, then the STM will restart the transaction using the latest value, and from there we will know whether the removal of the specified amount can proceed safely or not.

■ **Note**   Take some time to really review the preceding piece of code; don't rush through it. Make sure you understand what's happening, and when, in the context of multiple threads.

---

commute

The commute function provides us a "last one in wins" behavior when mutating a specified reference, and is most useful when you want the highest possible concurrency and the order of operations does not matter (transactions are designed to prevent multiple simultaneous writes to a ref).

In essence, commute will immediately return the result of applying the provided function on the reference, but at the end of the transaction it will perform the calculation again synchronously, and it is at *that* point it actually updates the reference's value. The modification itself is commutative, and so no transaction is ever rolled back.

This is why, in Listing 8-27, you could see the same value printed multiple times when executing that example code, but the actual end result is always consistent.

Listing 8-27. Example of Using commute

```
(def foo (ref 0))

(defn inc-ref [r]
  (dosync
    (commute r inc)
    (println @r)))

(let [threads (for [x (range 0 20)] (Thread. #(inc-ref foo)))]
  (doall (map #(.start %) threads))
  (doall (map #(.join %) threads))
  (inc-ref foo))
```

■ **Note**   We use Thread. instead of a future so that we can have greater control over when the thread is actioned, as well as to indicate that we wish to wait for all the threads to finish before we move on.

If you ran the code from Listing 8-27 but modified it so that you used alter instead of commute, then you would notice how alter enforces the order of updates, and so the printed values are always exactly counted 1-21 (whereas commute's end result is still 21, but the process to get there is commutative).

Channels

Now that we've covered all the standard core library concurrency features, there is one more item to consider, and that's the use of *channels*, which are only available within the core.async library.

To use core.async, you'll need to tell Leiningen to load it (similar to what we did in a previous chapter with core.match). The easiest way to do this right now–as we're still running all our examples within the REPL–is to stop the REPL you currently have open (press <Ctrl-d> to do that) and create the following project.clj file (or add the new lines if you already have a project.clj file). See Listing 8-28.

Listing 8-28. Update Project with core.async Dependency

```
(defproject test "0.1.0-SNAPSHOT"
  :dependencies [[org.clojure/clojure "1.8.0"]
                 [org.clojure/core.async "0.3.442"]]])
```

Once this file has been created, start up the REPL again using lein repl (Leiningen will use the content of the project.clj to set up its environment) and execute the line in Listing 8-29.

Listing 8-29. Load core.async into Your Running REPL Instance

```
(require '[clojure.core.async :as async :refer :all])
```

■ **Note**   Again, don't worry about understanding the syntax of either the project file or the require function call, as I'll explain all this soon enough when we start discussing Leiningen in more detail in a later chapter.

At this point, you'll have a group of macros available (such as <!!, >!!, chan, buffer, and more) at your disposal.

The idea behind core.async was borrowed from golang[2] (Google's own popular programming language, whose concurrency primitives are highly touted among the developer community).

Although Go has done the hard work of making the concept of channels popular in our modern age, the design of channels goes way back to the 1970s, starting with a paper called "Communicating Sequential Processes" (CSP) written by Tony Hoare.

---

[2]http://www.golang.org/

Effectively, a channel is a pipe: you stick data in one end and you pull it out from the other end. The reason this works really well, from a concurrency perspective, is because it protects the data on the way down the pipe from interference from other threads/processes.

Probably the most challenging part of using channels is the idea that they block your application when you put/pull data. This is because fundamentally they're connecting different processes. We'll almost always use channels with another concept known as a *go block*. But I'll come back to that; first, I think a simple example is in order. See Listing 8-30.

■ **Note**   The following code will block your running process indefinitely. You can press <Ctrl-c> while inside the REPL to break the block, but when designing your application, it would be wise to be mindful that channels can block a process if not set up properly.

Listing 8-30. Simple Example of a Channel That Will Block

```
(def c (chan))

(>!! c :foo)
;; will block until something

;; takes :foo out the other end of the channel
```

In Listing 8-30, we can see we've created a variable c and assigned it a new chan (channel). Once we have this channel, we can use >!! for putting a value into the channel, and we can use <!! for taking a value from the channel.

The problem with the preceding example is that it will block indefinitely once you call <!!. Ideally, what you'll want to do (at least for a workable example) is to use another thread for putting a value onto a channel, because at least the new thread spawned can be blocked, rather than blocking your main thread and causing the REPL to lock up!

Listing 8-31 demonstrates a slightly more practical example that doesn't block your REPL.

Listing 8-31. Simple Example of a Channel That Doesn't Block

```
(def c (chan))

(future (>!! c :foo))
;; this thread will be blocked

(<!! c)
;; :foo
```

In Listing 8-31, we put a message into the channel (in this case, the message is the keyword :foo), and because that's done in a child thread (thanks to the use of a future), we're able to continue working in the REPL's parent thread. From here, you can see we're now pulling whatever value is available from the channel (using <!!), and because the value is available we do not block.

So, for example, let's now say I want to try to pull another value from my channel c. Well, I've already pulled out the value :foo, and I know there is nothing left to take from the channel, so what will happen? Well, if I were to pull again (e.g., (<!! c)), that would block my entire thread until I had some code somewhere else in my program that pushed a value into the channel (causing my pull to unblock).

To avoid that issue (again, for the purposes of experimentation within the REPL), we can take advantage of futures again. See an example in Listing 8-32.

Listing 8-32. Place Value into Channel via future

```
(future
  (prn (str "hey! a new value " (<!! c)))) ;; blocks in a child thread

(>!! c "bar")
;; true (+ side effect: "hey! a new value bar" printed)
```

Go Blocks

The problem with using a future with channels is that a future gets its thread from a thread pool. So, there are a limited number of threads to begin with.

If you block a thread using a push/pull from a channel, then that's one less thread available for multi-threading your workload.

■ **Note** Futures share a thread pool with agents.

Clojure's core.async library also provides a go function that acts like an asynchronous wrapper: the body you provide to a go block will be executed asynchronously on a separate thread, and it's from a thread pool dedicated to just go blocks.

OK, so you have a separate thread pool with go blocks, but how does it differ from futures? Well, when using go you are able to "park" a thread rather than block it.

What *parking* means is that the process is removed from the thread, allowing the thread to be utilized by another go block process. When the other process has completed, it is placed back onto the thread to finish up (see Listing 8-33 for an example).

Listing 8-33. Simple Example of a go Block

```
(go
  (Thread/sleep 1000)
  (dotimes [x 5] (prn x)))

(prn "I wasn't blocked")
;; this is printed immediately (followed by the numbers 0-4)
```

When using channels from within a go block, you need to be aware that the syntax for pushing and pulling values is slightly different compared to when using channels outside of it (this is because of what we mentioned earlier about parking a go block, rather than blocking the thread it's running within).

The syntax for a channel push/pull is >!! and <!!, but when working with channels from within a go block, the syntax changes to <! and >!, which results in parking the process. This means the threads from the go thread pool can be reused while the existing go processes are blocked. See Listing 8-34.

Listing 8-34. Using go Blocks with Channels

```
(def c (chan))

(go
  (dotimes [x 10]
    (Thread/sleep 1000)
    (>! c x))) ;; every second we put a new number into the channel

(go
  (while true
    (prn (<! c)))) ;; forever pull content from the channel and print it
```

In Listing 8-34, we end up printing the values 0 to 9, one number per second. Another difference between a future and a go block is that you can access the return value of a future, whereas with a go block you'll always be returned a channel type, which is passed the last executed expression (see Listing 8-35).

Listing 8-35. Go Blocks Return a Channel Type

```
(def f (future (inc 1)))

@f
;; 2

(def g (go (inc 1)))
;; ManyToManyChannel

(<!! g)
;; 2
```

Thread Function

Now, you may wonder how many more async mechanisms Clojure can provide? Well, core.async also gives us the thread function. Effectively, it allows us to execute code in another thread (nothing new there, much like go and future), and it also returns a channel with the last expression put into the channel (again like go, so nothing extra there).

The only real difference is that the thread is pulled from an "unbounded" thread pool (meaning it has a theoretically unlimited number of threads it can create).

The use case for (thread) will be when you have a long-running process that potentially could block for a long time, causing your thread pool to be blocked if you had used a go block instead. But remember that creating threads is an expensive operation, and that is the benefit thread pools provide.

119

> ■ **Note**   When I first started looking at Clojure, I was overwhelmed by the number of concurrency mechanisms it provided. It wasn't until I really understood the problem space that it became clear all these mechanisms did actually serve a purpose and had a reason for existing.

Distinction

What's not normally made very clear though, is when you should even use channels. It would seem the rule of thumb is as follows:

- Create a thread (using future) if you need to make a synchronous process asynchronous.

- If the API or code you're using is already asynchronous, then use a go block.

I've yet to find an example that doesn't quite fit (in the work I use Clojure for at least), but your mileage may vary.

Before we move on, there are a few remaining interesting features core.async provides:

- alt!/alt!!

- buffered channels

- sliding/dropping channel buffers

- timeouts

Alternate

Let's start with the alt function (which I believe stands for *alternate*? As you'll see, it will alternate between the provided channels).

The alt! (parking) variation must be called from within a go block, while the alt!! variation can be called from outside (similar to >! vs >!!). You pass the alt! function a collection of channels, and whichever channel gets a value first is the one returned (see Listing 8-36).

Listing 8-36. Example of Using alt!! Function

```
(def a (chan))
(def b (chan))
(def c (chan))

(defn put-data [c n]
  (go (Thread/sleep (rand 10))
      (>! c (str "Hi " n))))

(put-data a "A")
(put-data b "B")
(put-data c "C")
```

```
(let [[result channel] (alts!! [a b c])]
    (prn "Result: " result)
    (prn "Channel: " channel))
```

In Listing 8-36, we create three separate channels and a function called put-data, which sleeps for a non-deterministic amount of time before putting a value into the provided channel.

Then we have a let block that acquires the result (and the channel it was produced from) and prints it. We use alt!! to ascertain which channel received a value first (the other results are discarded).

Buffered Channels

The next item we'll cover are buffered channels (and their variations: sliding and dropping). Channels by default are unbuffered, so up until this point when we've created a channel, if you were to push a single value in, then the channel would become full and your thread would be blocked until the value is pulled out of the channel.

To allow for greater concurrency, you can create your channel with a predefined buffer space. With a buffer of, let's say, five, you could push five values onto the channel without blocking. See Listing 8-37.

Listing 8-37. Example of a Buffered Channel

```
(def c (chan 5))

(def v [:a :b :c :d])

(dotimes [i 4]
    (>!! c (nth v i))
    (prn "Put " (nth v i) " into the channel. Next..."))
```

In Listing 8-37, if we hadn't given a buffer size of 5 to the channel when it was created, then the very first call to >!! would've blocked our REPL's thread indefinitely until we had either killed the running process or had a place defined in code already that would've extracted the values from the channel for us.

Sliding/Dropping Buffered Channels

We can take the buffered channel concept one step further with Clojure and utilize either a sliding buffer or a dropping buffer, depending on the needs of your application.

A *sliding* buffer is one that will drop the first buffered value when another value is pushed into the channel (structurally, this is a queue, but queues do not automatically drop elements; this is what Clojure's abstraction provides for us). A *dropping* buffer is one that drops the last buffered value when another value is pushed into the channel.

In both cases, neither channel will result in putting a value blocking your current thread, because of the way the channel handles buffer overflow. See Listing 8-38 for an example.

Listing 8-38. Example of Sliding and Dropping Buffers

```
(def s (chan (sliding-buffer 5)))

(def d (chan (dropping-buffer 5)))

(def v [:a :b :c :d :e :f :g :h :i :j])

(dotimes [i 10]
  (>!! s (nth v i))
  (prn "Put " (nth v i) " into the 'sliding buffer' channel"))

(dotimes [i 10]
  (>!! d (nth v i))
  (prn "Put " (nth v i) " into the 'dropping buffer' channel"))

(<!! s) ;; :f
(<!! d) ;; :a
```

In Listing 8-38, we're demonstrating both a sliding buffer and a dropping buffer. We create the different buffer types and pass those as arguments when creating our channels. Then, we create a loop whereby we stick ten values into the channels, and yet the channels can only hold a maximum of five values. So, we'll see how each type of buffer handles this problem.

With the sliding buffer, if we take a value from the channel we can see we get back :f first. This shows the first five values (:a, :b, :c, :d, :e) were pushed out when the next set of values was pushed in. As the name suggests, the channel contents are sliding older values out first.

With the dropping buffer, if we take a value from the channel we can see we get back :a first. This shows the last five values (:f, :g, :h, :i, :j) were dropped the moment the buffer became full. It's like the entrance to a very busy nightclub: the doorman will turn you away once the club becomes full.

■ **Note**   It seems that within the community most developers create unbounded channels, so one-in-one-out, and only utilize sliding/dropping buffers when they need to eke out as much performance and throughput as possible.

Timeout Channels

This is the last feature within the realm of concurrency I want to share with you and is a common pattern when utilizing channels: the use of a timeout channel to short-circuit potential zombie (or long-blocking) processes. See Listing 8-39.

Listing 8-39. Example of Timeout Channels

```
(def c (chan))

(let [[result channel]
      (alts!! [c (timeout 5000)])]
  (if result
    (prn "Result: " result)
    (prn "Timed out: " result))) ;; "Timed out: " nil
```

In Listing 8-39, we create a channel and then never send anything to it. We then use alts!! to try to take a value from the channel, but instead of being blocked indefinitely—because we can pass a collection of channels and the one that gets a value first is the one returned by alts!!—we are blocked initially for five seconds, and then the process unlocks and we get the result of nil.

This works because the timeout channel is an active channel for the set period of time, and then it sends itself a value of nil, which allows the alt!! to jump into action and subsequently short-circuit itself.

Summary

In this chapter, we've learned a *lot* of different techniques and tools for handling concurrent/multi-threaded code. We've looked at everything: delays, futures, promises, atoms, locks, agents, refs, and channels. Don't rush this chapter; go back and try all the examples and ensure you understand the concepts fully.

In the next chapter, we will look at namespaces and how we can utilize them for organizing and categorizing our code. Namespaces are a powerful feature that is prevalent in all Clojure code bases.

CHAPTER 9

Namespaces

Namespaces are a feature that allows the categorization of functions, symbols, and variables into well-defined groups. Later on in this chapter we'll see that namespaces can also be translated and mapped to an actual file system directory structure.

Let's start by using the REPL to demonstrate a simple example of how namespaces work. When we run lein repl we're automatically dropped into a new user namespace, and that namespace is pre-loaded with the Clojure core library. You can tell what namespace you're in by looking at the REPL console, which displays the current namespace just before your cursor position: user=>.

■ **Note** If you need to reference the namespace programmatically, then you can use the *ns* variable.

Now, let's see how we can create a new namespace foo.bar and then define a variable assigned to the symbol baz inside that new namespace. We'll then define a different value for baz back in the user namespace and see what happens when we reference the variable from the different namespaces.

Listing 9-1. Example of Creating a New Namespace

```
(ns foo.bar)
(def baz 1)
baz
;; 1

(ns user)
(def baz 2)
baz
;; 2

(ns foo.bar)
baz
;; 1
```

In Listing 9-1, you can see we've used the ns macro to create the foo.bar namespace. If the namespace already exists (such as was the case with the user namespace in Listing 9-1), then calling the ns macro and passing it a symbol that maps to a pre-existing namespace will instead move you into the specified namespace without creating it first.

So, in the preceding example, we first create the foo.bar namespace and then define baz to have the value 1. We then move back into the user namespace and define baz, but this time with a different value—2.

You can see from this example how we can safely define variables and functions with different behaviors and values depending on the namespace in which they are defined and contained.

What Is a Namespace?

Clojure's namespaces are really just a global map of symbols to variables/classes. Each namespace class can also contain its own mappings (mostly symbols to variables). The current namespace is stored in a Namespace object and is associated with the dynamic variable *ns*.

■ **Note** By default, the user namespace, and subsequently any namespace created using the ns macro, will have all functions from the clojure.core namespace (as well as the classnames from the java.lang namespaces) mapped and pre-loaded for them.

You can verify this from within the REPL by creating a new namespace using in-ns (rather than ns). The in-ns function will create a namespace *without* the clojure.core namespace pre-loaded. See Listing 9-2 for an example that demonstrates how the new namespace will be missing the default namespaces.

Listing 9-2. New Namespace with in-ns Will Be Missing clojure.core

```
(in-ns 'beep)
;; beep namespace doesn't exist
;; so this created it and moved us inside the namespace

(loaded-libs)
;; this function is located in clojure.core
;; the clojure.core namespace hasn't been pre-loaded
;; so this will display an error in the REPL

(clojure.core/refer 'clojure.core)
;; we explictly load the clojure.core namespace

(loaded-libs)
;; we now successfully execute the function
```

Loading Namespaced Files

If you're testing an existing application from the REPL and you're looking to load a code file that requires some other dependencies, then you'll want to use the load function. The load function attempts to find the given path in your "classpath" and then load that file. The classpath is what Java uses to identify the location of code libraries, and because Clojure is built upon Java it means we need to ensure our classpath has the relevant paths added to it.

The project management tool Leiningen handles the adding of dependencies and libraries to our classpath via a project.clj file. So as long as you have your dependencies listed there you should be able to use the load function to pull them into a REPL session. See Listing 9-3 for an example of the load function.

Listing 9-3. Loading Code from External Files

```
(load "/path/to/namespace")
(in-ns 'namespace)
```

Now, the reason you use load *before* in-ns is because even though you might have a file that defines the specified namespace, the REPL won't be able to locate it unless you add it to the JVM classpath. The load function adds the namespace to the classpath.

■ **Note**   Make sure the path starts with a forward slash and that it's relative to Leiningen's src directory (see the next note); this is because the Leiningen tool messes with your OS' JVM classpath for each Leiningen project.

Although we've yet to look at the Leiningen project-automation tool, it's worth mentioning that part of a Clojure project's setup requires the use of a project.clj file that bootstraps the application.

If you want to follow along with what I'm about to explain, it's probably easier if you exit the REPL and then run the following command from your terminal: lein new compojure-app foo. This will generate a new project for you. Move into that new project directory (cd foo), and you'll find there is a new project.clj.

Spend some time looking around the organization of folders and files in this new Leiningen project. Don't worry for now about what it all means or how it works, as we'll be covering that in a later chapter. But namespaces play an important role in setting up a real-world Clojure application, and so this will give you a basic starting point to help you understand the following information.

One of the settings within the project.clj bootstrap file is a :handler key, which informs Leiningen of which Clojure file is the entry point for the application (there is also a :init function that executes just before the handler).

■ **Note**   For most Leiningen project templates, you'll find your Clojure code located at: src/<name_of_project>/<file.clj>.

For example, if your project.clj includes :handler foo.handler/app, you're effectively telling Leiningen to locate the entry point at src/foo/handler.clj (and within that file you would find the app function that bootstraps your application).

When running lein repl from the project directory, you can execute (ns foo.handler) to jump into the namespace and start executing the functions exposed by that namespace. See Listing 9-4 for a simple example.

Listing 9-4. Loading Namespace into the REPL

```
(ns foo.handler)
(init) ;; foo is starting
```

If you make a change to a file—for example, let's say you update the handler.clj file with a new variable: (def x 123)— in order for that change to be reflected within the current REPL instance that's already running, you would be required to reload the namespace file. See Listing 9-5.

Listing 9-5. Reload Namespace into the REPL

```
(load "/foo/handler")
x ;; 123
```

If you want to display all the namespaces that have been loaded, then the simplest option is to use the (loaded-libs) function. If you were to run that command within the current REPL instance, you would see a big list of namespaces loaded for you (including any new namespaces that were added after the REPL was started). See Listing 9-6.

Listing 9-6. Loaded Libraries Within Current REPL Instance

```
#{clj-stacktrace.core clj-stacktrace.repl clj-stacktrace.utils clj-time.
core clj-time.format clojure.core.protocols clojure.core.server clojure.edn
clojure.instant clojure.java.browse clojure.java.io clojure.java.javadoc ...}
```

Interning

We covered variables way back in Chapter 2, and at that point I stated:

> *Variables are not available within other namespaces unless they are "interned" into them. Interning is a fancy way of saying "find variable x within this current namespace; and if it doesn't exist then create it". But you can also "intern" variables from another namespace using the :refer feature of the ns macro.*
>
> —Me, Chapter 2

So, let's take a look at the different ways we can "intern" data from another namespace. There are a few different options:

- `:use`
- `:require`
  - `:as`
  - `:refer`
  - `:all`

Now, I should actually clarify that there are really only two ways to intern data, and that is by using the first two items in the preceding list (`:use` and `:require`). The other items in the list are all subset features related to `:require` and are referred to in the official documentation as *libspecs*.

■ **Note**   I'm going to cover `:use` last because it's considered unnecessary now that `:require`'s functionality has vastly improved since the earlier releases of Clojure. I'm covering `:use` just so you know that it existed first, but it's no longer needed, as `:require`'s functionality supersedes it.

I'll begin by explaining how each of these items works, along with their differences, but before I do I would like to take a small detour...

Root Bindings

It's important when talking about variables to understand that they also have something called a *root binding* and are known to be "thread-local." What this means in practical terms is that when you create a variable and assign it a value—e.g., (def foo "hello")— its root binding is the value you've defined (in this case, the string "hello"). Once you associate a value with a variable, then that becomes the "root binding" for the variable, and it means that any threads created from within the current namespace will all have access to it, as they are essentially created within the same memory space. This is what's meant by "thread-local", other namespaces won't be able to see that variable or its value.

If you define a variable but don't assign it a value, then it is considered "unbound" (see Listing 9-7 for an example).

Listing 9-7. Example of an Unbound Variable

```
(def foo)

foo
;; #<Unbound Unbound: #'user/foo>
```

Dynamic Variables

We covered dynamic variables back in Chapter 2 (i.e., the ^:dynamic attribute and the binding form), but as we're now reading a chapter about namespaces, it would be pertinent for me to mention a point that might not have made sense if referenced right at the start of the book: the reason the ns macro is able to dynamically change the namespace in Clojure is because the macro modifies the global *ns* variable, meaning it is possible for it to be redefined.

▪ **Note**   The convention for defining dynamic variables is to wrap them in "ear muffs" (i.e., asterisks). For example, *var_name*.

Detour Over...

OK, back to the discussion of interning and the list of items we had earlier (i.e., :use, :require, etc.). I'll be using a new application. Earlier, we actually created a simple web server application using lein new compojure-app <name>. Now we'll use lein new app <name>.

▪ **Note**   The difference is that the latter example is a "standard" application rather than a web server. We'll discuss the different types of applications in a future chapter covering the Leiningen tool in more detail.

Similar to the previous application, if you look at the project.clj file you'll find a structure that resembles what we saw before. The difference here is that instead of a :handler key we'll find a :main key. But it does the same thing—it tells Leiningen where the main code file can be located.

In this example, we'll see the main file is set to foo.core, but I'm also going to create some new files, foo/bar.clj and foo/baz.clj, which will in turn represent the namespaces foo.bar and foo.baz. I'll demonstrate each of these files as we go through the examples.

▪ **Note**   The use of core as a file name (and namespace) within project.clj is simply convention. There's no reason why you couldn't rename the core file to something else and manually update project.clj to reflect the new file/namespace.

The syntax used in the following examples (see Listings 9-8, 9-9, and 9-10) is specific to Clojure code files. If you wanted to test these features in the REPL, then you could call them as direct functions. For example, where we have defined something like (:use name.space) you could change it to (use 'name.space) within the REPL.

> ■ **Note**   When using the functions directly (as opposed to using them from within the ns macro), you'll need to quote any symbols/vectors used.

Let's now imagine that each of our namespaces (foo.core, foo.bar, and foo.baz) contains the code from Listings 9-8, 9-9, and 9-10 (I would suggest you edit your test foo app to mimic the following examples if you wish to follow along in your REPL).

foo.core

Listing 9-8. The foo.core Namespace Code

```
(ns foo.core
  (:use foo.bar)
  (:use foo.baz)
  (:gen-class))

(def x 1)

(defn -main [& args]
  (println "Hello, World!"))
```

foo.bar

Listing 9-9. The foo.bar Namespace Code

```
(ns foo.bar)

(def a 1)
(def b 2)

(defn beep [] "bop")
(defn- bing [] "bong")
```

> ■ **Note**   You might have noticed in foo.bar the function bing defined using defn-. The extra hyphen at the end is important, as it means that when generating a Java class from that namespace it'll treat that function as private and so it won't be available within the other namespace.

foo.baz

Listing 9-10. The foo.baz Namespace Code

```
(ns foo.baz)

(def c 3)
(def d 4)
(def e 5)
```

Let's start up our REPL (lein repl) from within the new foo directory, and we should notice we're dropped into the same namespace as specified by the :main attribute in project.clj (you should see the line in the terminal set to foo.core=>).

From the main namespace foo.core you should be able to enter into the REPL the symbols a, b, c, d, and e and see the corresponding values assigned to them. Equally, you should be able to execute the function (beep) and see the appropriate return value.

But, you won't be able to execute the (bing) function, as it was defined using defn- and so should be private and only accessible via the foo.bar namespace. Listing 9-11 demonstrates how to access it.

Listing 9-11. Access Private Function by Entering its Namespace

```
(in-ns 'foo.bar)
(bing) ;; "bong"
```

Now that we have a better understanding of how namespaces are working with our foo application, let's go back and look at the :require, :as, :refer, :all, and :use features and see how they work.

:require

The inclusion of :require within an ns macro means that it will import any public variables into the current namespace, and from there the options available (:as and :refer) help to determine *how* you access the imported data (as we'll see in the next couple of sections). The syntax structure for :require is as shown in Listing 9-12.

Listing 9-12. Syntax Structure for :require Macro

```
(ns <namespace>
  (:require <namespace>
            [<namespace> :refer [<public_var_1> <public_var_2>]]
            [<namespace> :as <shorter_name>]
            [<namespace> :as <shorter_name> :refer [<public_var>]])
  (:gen-class))
```

:as

The :as libspec allows you to rename the namespace itself.

We've already seen the shorthand form of :require, but you can write it the *long-form* way if you prefer (see Listing 9-13).

Listing 9-13. Long-form Version of :require

```
(ns foo.core
  (:require [clojure.string :as str])
  (:require [foo.bar :as fbr])
  (:require [foo.baz :as fbz])
  (:gen-class))
```

However, it's actually more than likely you'll want to use the short-form variation instead (see Listing 9-14). This means you can refer to all the public vars inside the foo.bar and foo.baz namespaces using a shorter symbol. For example, instead of writing foo.bar/b (to access the public b variable) you can type fbr/b.

Listing 9-14. Short-form Version of :require

```
(ns foo.core
  (:require [clojure.string :as str]
            [foo.bar :as fbr]
            [foo.baz :as fbz])
  (:gen-class))
```

■ **Note** When using the function version of require (i.e., outside of the ns macro), the quote before the vector means you don't have to quote each symbol inside the vector. For example, (require '[name.space :as nmsp]) instead of (require ['name.space : as 'nmsp]).

:refer

The :refer libspec allows you to import only the public variables you need into the current scope. All other public variables are still available, but you have to provide a fully qualified namespace to access them. See Listing 9-15.

Listing 9-15. Example of the :refer Libspec

```
(ns foo.core
  (:require clojure.string
            [foo.bar :refer [a beep]]
            [foo.baz :as fbz :refer [c]])
  (:gen-class))
```

In Listing 9-15, we can see that we're loading the `clojure.string` namespace as is; we're not shortening it in any way. So, if we wanted to use the `upper-case` function from that namespace, then we would execute (`clojure.script/upper-case` "make me upper case!"), which would subsequently return "MAKE ME UPPER CASE!".

In the second statement [`foo.bar :refer [a beep]`], we're saying "make a and beep available in the current scope and everything else that's public from that namespace we'll have to access via the full namespace." So, typing a will return 2; typing (beep) will return "bop", and to access b we can't just type that, but instead must type `foo.bar/b`, which will return 1.

In the third statement [`foo.baz :as fbz :refer [c]`], we're saying the same sort of thing as before, but now we're also stating that when we have to refer to a public variable using the full namespace, we only have to use the shortened fbz as the namespace rather than the longer `foo.baz`. So, if you type c you'll get back 3, and if you want to access d or e then you'll need to type `fbz/d` and `fbz/e` instead.

■ **Note**   With the third statement form, you can still use the long-form namespace. So, both `fbz/c` and `foo.baz/c` work.

:all

The `:all` libspec works in conjunction with `:refer`. So, whereas with `:refer` you would provide a collection of symbols that represent the public variables you want to import into the current namespace, you can instead provide `:all` as an option in place of the collection.

Listing 9-16. Example of :all Libspect

```
(ns foo.core
  (:require clojure.string
            [foo.bar :refer :all])
  (:gen-class))
```

In Listing 9-16, we would be able to reference a, b, and beep in the current namespace without having to provide a fully qualified namespace. For example, we wouldn't have to specify `foo.bar/a`; we could just use a).

■ **Note**   You'll notice in the next section that `:all` is effectively the default usage of `:use`, hence its deprecation.

:use

The inclusion of :use within the ns macro means that it will import any public variables into the current namespace and overwrite any existing definitions with the same name as those being imported. Remember that functions are also assigned to variables underneath the defn macro, so public functions are also made available/overridden within the current namespace.

You'll notice an issue with using :use if you change the variable c in foo.baz to be a variable that's already defined in another namespace (like var a from foo.bar).

Try changing (def c 3) to (def a 3) and then running lein repl from the root of the project. You should see the first few lines of in the REPL output as showing an exception (see Listing 9-17).

Listing 9-17. Exception Raised When Mixing Variables with :use

```
a already refers to #'foo.bar/a in namespace foo.core.
```

The exception occurs because foo.baz is trying to redefine the variable a, which was defined already by foo.bar. This is the issue with using the standard use without one of its libspec options, such as :exclude, :only, or :rename.

■ **Note**   When calling use from the REPL (e.g., (use 'foo.baz)) it'll redefine any definitions without warning.

To fix the exception (and subsequently allow all our code to load and function properly) we need to make a decision about what we want to do with regards to importing the foo.baz namespace.

We could exclude the a and d variables, or we could use :only to pull in the e variable by itself (which in this example makes more sense, as it's less typing); or we could even rename c and d using :rename. The choice is up to you.

But let's say we decide to pull in the a variable. This means we'll need :only and :rename. We can see an example of this in Listing 9-18 where we pull in the a variable from foo.baz and rename it to new-a. Using this format, we can pull in all the dependencies we need without worrying about any conflicts.

Listing 9-18. Use :only to Pull Specific Variables

```
(ns foo.core
  (:use foo.bar)
  (:use [foo.baz :only [d] :rename {a new-a}])
  (:gen-class))
```

Anything Else?

Although I'm not aiming for completeness, it's probably worth mentioning a couple more things. The first is that you have another macro you can use in place of the ns macro (we actually saw it earlier, but I purposely didn't clarify). It's called in-ns. The only real difference between them is that in-ns doesn't provide access to any libspecs (i.e., :use, :require, :as, :refer, or :all).

The second thing worth mentioning is the use of the libspecs :verbose, :reload, and :reload-all. These only apply to the require function and its ns variation (:require ...). For example, if were to add :verbose, then Clojure would print out any information regarding calls to the load function. This can help to clarify what the :require calls are doing internally by displaying the underlying calls being made.

The :reload libspec ensures that even if a library has been loaded (e.g., loaded by another namespace), it should be loaded again in case of any changes. I've not had a reason to use this behavior myself, with the exception of when I'm playing around in the REPL and constantly loading dependencies over and over. The :reload-all libspec works the same way, but it recursively checks all dependencies for all loaded libraries.

One last item would be the import command, which is useful for importing Java classes and interfaces. Listing 9-19 demonstrates a basic example of its usage.

Listing 9-19. Example of Importing a Java Class

```
(import java.util.Date)
(def now (Date.))
(str now) ;; "Thu Jun 29 09:24:04 BST 2017"
```

Summary

In this chapter, we've learned about the various namespace symbols and macros, how to create new namespaces dynamically within the REPL, as well as how to move between existing namespaces and execute code within those spaces. Probably most important, we've understood how to intern variables across namespaces and how to avoid conflicts via the various libspec options available to us.

In the next chapter, we're going to look at how to manipulate the Clojure language itself by utilizing a feature known as macros. This is a powerful feature and one that we must take care with, lest we add complexity and confusion to our codebases.

CHAPTER 10

■ ■ ■

Macros

Arguably one of the most interesting features of Clojure is its ability to provide functionality that allows the user to redefine the language and add their own features that aren't available by default. I mean, how many times have you written some code (in whatever language, but let's say JavaScript) and thought "I really wish I had feature X from language Y"?

With a language such as JavaScript, I'm willing to bet that happens a lot. I'm sure there will be some JavaScript developers who would counter with a point about compilers being available that let you compile valid ES7 code down to ES5 code (for example). But that still doesn't account for compiling ES5 code down to ES3, which in some situations you can't even do (because of restrictions in the ES3 language specification). Not to mention there are now two sets of compilation steps to make sure your code actually works across as wide a range of devices as possible.

■ **Note** Progressive enhancement[1] can help the situation, but the work involved with implementing progressive enhancement is not trivial, and compared with having native support within the language to facilitate redefining the language, that's an immensely powerful concept.

But even if you are a JS developer and are able to take advantage of one of the popular compilers available, maybe you can't find a compiler that offers you the *features* that you want. In that situation, you might end up stumbling across something like SweetJS,[2] which is a compiler that allows you to define your own features. But this introduces yet another barrier to getting work done, as you have an external dependency to manage.

The ability to utilize Clojure's macro feature allows the core Clojure library to stay compact and focused while allowing developers to add their own features to the language with the safety of knowing that the macro system is natively part of the language and not some external tool that could potentially end up unsupported.

---

[1]https://en.wikipedia.org/wiki/Progressive_enhancement
[2]http://sweetjs.org/

© Mark McDonnell 2017
M. McDonnell, *Quick Clojure*, DOI 10.1007/978-1-4842-2952-1_10

■ **Note**   The Clojure authors have demonstrated (a few times in the past) a habit of assimilating popular abstractions built using the macro system back into the official Clojure codebase. This means if you create something useful using macros, then your work could eventually end up being used by all Clojure devs.

Let's start our understanding of macros by reviewing two specific macros that we've already used in previous chapters and that are part of the core Clojure library: -> and ->>.

Listing 10-1. Examples of the -> and ->> Macros

```
(->  6 (/ 2) (+ 10))
;; 13

(->> 6 (/ 2) (+ 10))
;; 31/3
```

In Listing 10-1, we have two lines of code that are very similar and yet return very different values. The only difference between the two lines is the extra chevron character > on the second line. This extra character causes the equation to change, but how?

In Clojure, -> is known as the "thread first" macro, while ->> is known as the "thread last" macro. For the thread first macro, the first argument (i.e., 6 in our example) is passed as the first argument to each function call that follows. For the thread last macro, the first argument (again, 6 in our example) is passed as the last argument to each function call that follows.

To more clearly visualize how the macro system works, we can utilize a function called macroexpand to show us the long-form version of the macro (basically, it displays what we would have written ourselves if the macro system didn't exist).

Listing 10-2. Expanding a Macro Using macroexpand

```
(macroexpand '(->  6 (/ 2) (+ 10)))
;; (+ (/ 6 2) 10)

(macroexpand '(->> 6 (/ 2) (+ 10)))
;; (+ 10 (/ 2 6))
```

To use the macroexpand function, as seen in Listing 10-2, we needed to provide it the expression we were running earlier. But how do we prevent those expressions from actually being executed and the *result* of the expressions being passed to macroexpand? Well, the solution is to quote the expression, and we do this by placing a single quote before the first parenthesis of the expression form.

■ **Note**   We could have wrapped the expression in a function call to quote; e.g., (quote (-> 6 (/ 2) (+ 10))), but ' is more succinct.

So, we can see that by passing in '(-> 6 (/ 2) (+ 10)) we get (+ (/ 6 2) 10) back. The return value is the macro expanded, and, similarly, in the second line, if we pass in '(->> 6 (/ 2) (+ 10)) we get back the expanded result of (+ 10 (/ 2 6)).

Notice how with "thread first" (->) the first argument 6 is now the first argument to the division function / and that the result of calling that function is itself now the first expression passed to the call to the addition function +.

With "thread last" (->>), we have the first argument 6 passed as the last argument to the division function, and the result of calling that function is then passed into the + function as the last argument.

Expanding All the Way Down

The macroexpand function is useful for ensuring all macros within the quoted expression are expanded, but that doesn't include nested macros inside a macro. Let me explain by way of an example (see Listing 10-3).

Listing 10-3. Macroexpand Doesn't Include Nested Macros

```
(cond (even? 2) "even" :else "odd") ;; "even"
(cond (even? 1) "even" :else "odd") ;; "odd"

(macroexpand '(cond (even? 2) "even" :else "odd"))
;; (if (even? 2) "even" (clojure.core/cond :else "odd"))
```

In Listing 10-3, we have a cond macro that, when passed a predicate, will return either "even" or "odd" depending on the result of the predicate. In this case, if we pass in the value 2, then the return result is "even", and if we pass in 1, then the value falls through to the :else case, and so the return value becomes "odd".

As you can see from the result of the macroexpand function, we get back an expanded version of the cond macro. But we have an issue: the cond macro internally calls itself again, and so for us to see a truly representative expansion of the cond macro, we should use the macroexpand-all function instead.

To access the macroexpand-all function, you'll need to load it into the REPL from the clojure.walk namespace (as it's not part of the core namespace). The walk namespace is part of the standard Clojure language, so you don't need to update the project dependencies like you did with core.match and core.async. Instead, you use the require function either inside the REPL or from the top of your code file.

Listing 10-4. Requiring the clojure.walk Namespace

```
(require '[clojure.walk :as w])
```

Once you have loaded the clojure.walk namespace (see Listing 10-4) you should be able to reference the macroexpand-all function to fully expand the cond macro example from earlier. See Listing 10-5.

Listing 10-5. Expand cond Example with macroexpand-all

```
(w/macroexpand-all '(cond (even? 2) "even" :else "odd"))

;; (if (even? 2) "even" (if :else "odd" nil))
```

Writing Your Own Macros

There are five aspects to creating your own macro, and these depend on how complex the macro needs to be:

- Define the macro (defmacro)
- Quoting (')
- Syntax quoting (`)
- Unquoting (~)
- Unquote splicing (~@)
- Generating symbols (gensym, #)

Interestingly, items 2-5 are all usable from *outside* of a macro, and so I'm going to demonstrate those first. After that, I'm going to dissect a custom macro in order to understand how it works and what some of the typical challenges are that we can expect to face.

Quoting '

Back in Chapter 2, when we were looking at the list data structure, I noted that some readers might have been curious as to the point of the single quote in front of the list. As mentioned then, it is known as *quoting* the data structure so that the Clojure compiler doesn't attempt to evaluate it.

Listing 10-6. Quoting a List Data Structure to Prevent Evaluation

```
(def l '(1 2 3))

l
;; (1 2 3)
```

In Listing 10-6, you should notice that the value assigned to the variable l is actually a list data structure, (1 2 3), and not the *result* of the Clojure compiler trying to execute 1 as a function and passing 2, 3 as function arguments (which wouldn't have worked, as there is no such function in Clojure called 1).

Quoting is a useful feature to have for those times when, from an algorithm perspective, you really need to utilize a genuine linked list data structure (as opposed to a vector or set, for example).

■ **Note**   There are other ways to create a linked list data structure: (`list 1 2 3`) and (`quote (1 2 3)`) are two popular options, although the `quote` function can be used on any type of Clojure form.

Syntax Quoting `

Syntax quoting works the same as the standard quoting functionality, the only difference being it converts each expression into a fully qualified namespace.

Listing 10-7. Syntax Quoting Results in Fully Qualified Namespaces

```
(def l '(1 2 3))

`(+ l)

;; (clojure.core/+ user/l)
```

You can see in Listing 10-7 that we've first defined the l variable to be assigned a literal list data structure. From there, we've used a backtick (`) in front of our expression (+ l), and the result is a qualified namespaced version of that expression.

This means the + function becomes clojure.core/+ and the l variable becomes user/l (in this case, I executed the example code from within the REPL environment).

■ **Note**   If you tried to evaluate the resulting expression (`clojure.core/+ user /l`) you would find the code doesn't work. This is because we need to flatten (i.e., splat) the list elements so they are no longer contained within parentheses but are inlined arguments to the + function. I'll demonstrate how to do this shortly using the unquote splicing syntax.

Unquoting ~

When you quote an expression, it means we want the compiler to not evaluate it or any of its sub-expressions. But every now and then you'll want the majority of your expression to be quoted (i.e., not evaluated) and yet maybe some small nested parts *to be* evaluated still.

Listing 10-8. Evaluate Nested Expressions, but Not Entire Expression

```
(def l '(1 2 3))

`(+ ~l)

;; (clojure.core/+ (1 2 3))
```

What we can see in Listing 10-8 is that we've quoted the expression using a backtick, but then we've used the tilde character (~) to "unquote" the l variable so that it ends up being evaluated by the Clojure compiler. This means we now get a namespaced + function unevaluated, followed by the expression (1 2 3).

■ **Note** The output from Listing 10-8 is non-functional because the expression (1 2 3) is invalid. There is no function 1 found in the core namespace.

Unquote Splicing ~@

In the previous examples, we've demonstrated specific features that have produced non-functional results. Let's take a moment now to resolve that issue and to turn the next example into one that can execute successfully.

Listing 10-9. Splat Evaluated Sequence Using Unquote Splicing

```
(def l '(1 2 3))

`(+ ~@l)
;; (clojure.core/+ 1 2 3)

(clojure.core/+ 1 2 3)
;; 6

(eval `(+ ~@l))
;; 6
```

So, in Listing 10-9, we can see that we're using the backtick quoting syntax to ensure that our expression isn't evaluated. But in this example, we want the list data structure (the one assigned to the l variable) to not be placed next to the + function as a list, but instead placed there as individual arguments.

To achieve the goal of evaluating the list data structure (so it's not placed next to the + as user/l) and then flattening the list data structure, we utilize not the unquote tilde but the unquote splicing ~@. We can see this returns us (clojure.core/+ 1 2 3), which you can paste into your REPL and execute to see it produce the correct result of 6.

If you wanted to programmatically evaluate the result of the form `(+ ~@l) you would need to wrap it in a call to the eval function (as demonstrated in Listing 10-9).

■ **Note** You can't use unquote splicing without the quote backtick syntax, as this would make it very difficult for the Clojure compiler to understand what should or shouldn't be evaluated.

Generating Symbols gensym/#

When using macros, you may eventually stumble across the problem of variable bindings (both in the macro and in the containing local scope) conflicting with each other. To work around this issue, you can generate a unique symbol within the macro by utilizing the gensym function.

■ **Note**   It's important to realize that gensym will always return a fresh unique value, so you can also provide a prefix string that helps to identify the symbol while debugging.

Listing 10-10. Using gensym to Create Unique Identifier

```
(gensym)
;; G__791

(gensym "hello")
;; hello794

`hello#
;; hello__803__auto__
```

In Listing 10-10, the last example uses the # shorthand syntax for gensym, which means we're required to use the quote ` syntax; otherwise, the compiler won't know what to do (this is because a # is a valid character for a symbol).

It's also worth being aware that the # variation ensures the same identifier is used throughout the quoted expression, whereas each reference to gensym would be a new value.

Macro Dissection

At this point, we have a basic understanding of all the individual parts that can be used to create a dynamic and robust macro feature. Let's put this all together by reviewing a more complicated macro example-code snippet and understanding how it works.

Clojure doesn't have a classical for loop construct (and by "classical" I'm referring to a low-level language like C) whereby you specify a starting value, a condition, and an incrementor and subsequently loop until the specified condition is no longer met.

To remedy this within the Clojure language, let's implement this missing construct as a macro. The output from executing the following for-loop macro we're going to define should be the numbers zero through nine printed to stdout (one number per line).

■ **Note**   I would recommend spending a good amount of time reviewing Listing 10-11 to be sure you are able to put together all the different syntax we've seen so far.

Listing 10-11. A Custom for Loop Construct Built Using Macro Features

```
(defmacro for-loop [[sym init check change] & steps]
  `(loop [~sym ~init accumulated# nil]
     (if ~check
       (let [new-value# (do ~@steps)]
         (recur ~change new-value#))
       accumulated#)))

(for-loop [i 0, (< i 10), (inc i)]
  (prn i))
```

OK, so let's start by looking at how we called the for-loop macro. We can see that we're passing in a vector that contains our loop information: [i 0, (< i 10), (inc i)]. This is followed by a "body" expression, (prn i), which we expect to be executed on each loop iteration.

■ **Note** We could pass in multiple body expressions to be executed using this current macro implementation if we wanted. But for the sake of simplicity and demonstrating the basic functionality, we provided only one form to be evaluated per iteration.

Within the macro itself, we destructure the incoming vector (i.e., we extract each element from the incoming vector data structure) into the following local bindings:

- sym: i
- init: 0
- check: (< i 10)
- change: (inc 1)

We also take the remaining arguments, (prn i), which we assume to be the body to be executed on each iteration, and use & steps to assign them into a steps collection. This means it is constructed as a list, like so: ((prn i)).

At this point, we start to define the main body of our macro. In summary, we carry out the following steps:

- Create a loop (as a target for a later recur).
  - Bind the symbol i to the value 0.
  - Bind the dynamically generated symbol (i.e., accumulated#) to the value nil.
- Use an if statement to check if the local i value is less than 10.
  - The check condition was passed into the macro at runtime (i.e., (< i 10)).
  - The value will be less than 10 initially, as we've only just set it to 0 (see previous step).

- If the value is greater than or equal to 10, then the else statement returns the value assigned to accumulated#.

  - We'll see in a moment how accumulated# is updated each iteration to a new value.

- If the value IS less than 10, then we execute the provided body expression(s).

  - The return value from the last body expression is assigned to new-value#.

  - We then use recur to jump back to the start of the loop and pass in new values.

  - The new values passed in for each iteration are the result from executing the change expression (i.e., (inc i)).

  - Then accumulated# is passed the current value assigned to new-value#.

You can see from these steps that the main meat of the solution is the use of loop and recur to allow recursively executing code, and that for each recursion we pass in updated values that allow the logic within the loop to decide if it should recurse again or stop.

That's it, really, for understanding the basics of macros. You should now have enough information to go away and become dangerous . . . I mean, inspirational!

I also think it's probably worth my saying (although I'm regretting it already): "With great power, comes great responsibility"; and what we mean by this (in the context of writing macros in Clojure) is: There are subtle issues with using macros, especially if another solution exists without the need for macros. If you need something executed at compile time rather than runtime, then, fine, a macro will help. But first see if a standard function exists that would suffice.

■ **Note**   You can't pass a macro around within your code (e.g., as a function argument) the same way as you can with a standard function. This ultimately means you lose some composability within your code's design, which is a fundamental principle of functional programming.

Summary

In this chapter, we've delved a little deeper into the Lisp-style syntax in order to help us redefine what behaviors are available in Clojure. This concept (and its implementation) is extremely powerful, and there are many examples of macros in the core library (and in other standard Clojure namespaces).

I would recommend starting simple when creating macros, as well as spending a fair amount of time looking at the source code for existing Clojure-implemented macros (but also including those macros created by the wider Clojure community).

In the next chapter, we'll be focusing on object-oriented programming features available within the Clojure language. Remember that Clojure isn't a 100 percent strict functional language (like, say, the Haskell[3] programming language). Although we won't be diving into how to incorporate Java code with Clojure, the OOP features available in Clojure tie in nicely with the Java environment.

---

[3]https://www.haskell.org/

CHAPTER 11

■ ■ ■

Object Orientation

One of the confusing aspects of Clojure is that although it aims at being a functional programming language, it does also provide "object-oriented" features (*gasp*). This is similar to other programming languages, such as Scala,[1] which also provides both FP and OOP syntax.

When to use OOP in Clojure is a tricky discussion point and depends on the requirements of the project you're working on, and so we won't make any opinionated statements on that topic. Although, I will say, for me personally I like the structural aspect of some of the items we'll be looking at shortly, and it can also be valuable to use specific types to help build boundaries between different systems.

Ultimately, the OOP features within Clojure aren't as prominent as those found in other languages, and definitely not nearly as much as those found in Scala, which seems to aim for an even split.

In this chapter, there is a (small) select group of features that I will be covering, and they are as follows:

- `defprotocol`
- `deftype`
- `defrecord`
- `reify`

Java Interop

When using object-oriented features in Clojure, you'll eventually discover each has specific nuances that tie it to the underlying Java language/VM that Clojure uses as its host environment.

If you plan on working with OOP or interacting with Java libraries, then I recommend you both read the Clojure notes on the topic of interop with Java[2] as well as review the documentation for the macros/functions described in this chapter, as they go into more detail on how the different items are handled internally by Clojure (there are quite a few low-level configuration details that can be of interest to some readers, but are generally out of the scope of this book).

---

[1]https://www.scala-lang.org/
[2]https://clojure.org/reference/java_interop

© Mark McDonnell 2017
M. McDonnell, *Quick Clojure*, DOI 10.1007/978-1-4842-2952-1_11

defprotocol

The defprotocol macro is used alongside both of the following OOP types (defrecord and deftype), and its primary purpose is to create an interface.

If you're unfamiliar with the concept of an interface, its purpose is to define a contract that all objects guarantee to provide if they state their support of the specific interface.

Listing 11-1. Simple Interface Example with defprotocol

```
(defprotocol Foo
  (bar [this abc])
  (baz [this] [this abc]))
```

In Listing 11-1, we start by defining a new protocol called Foo (using the defprotocol macro). Within this block, we define two methods, bar and baz. This means any object that claims to support this interface must provide implementations for the specified functions along with their specific signatures.

The bar method accepts two arguments. The first is a parameter called this, and it should be the object instance we're calling the bar method upon (hence, we've used the traditional naming convention of this, as seen in many programming languages, such as Java), while the second argument is a parameter called abc.

We see a similar definition for the baz method. The only difference is that this method has "multiple arity," meaning that it can be called with either one or two arguments and we can define two separate behaviors depending on the number of arguments provided when calling the method.

■ **Note** definterface is a similar feature to defprotocol. The difference is that the former generates an actual interface .class that Java can utilize in order to pass valid objects to Clojure functions.

By itself, defprotocol isn't very useful, so let's move on to the next section, where we can see it being put to good use.

deftype

For us to be able to use the protocol (i.e., interface) we've defined, we'll need a concrete object (class instance) we can assign it to. This is where the macros deftype and defrecord come into focus.

Both deftype and defrecord will create an object, but which one you use will depend on subtle implementation details. For example, the deftype macro creates a bare-bones Java class instance that will allow for further Java inter-op and mutating of the internal data fields. However, defrecord (see the next section for more details) will act more like a simple immutable hash map.

Listing 11-2. Example of Using deftype

```
(deftype Qux [data]
  Foo
  (bar [this args]
    (prn (str "hello " (subs (str (class this)) 6)
              " from bar! I've been given: " args)))
  (baz [this]
    (prn (class this) data))
  (baz [this args]
    (prn (str "hello " (subs (str (class this)) 6)
              " from baz! I've been given: " args))))
```

OK, there's a lot going on in Listing 11-2, so let's break this down into chunks. First, we can see that we've defined a new type called Qux and specified that it accepts a single constructor argument called data.

The purpose of deftype is to ultimately produce a type that acts a lot like a typical Java class, and so in the following example (Listing 11-3) we'll see that when we initialize this type (class) we are able to pass in our own specific data to the constructor (which subsequently is referenced from inside the baz method).

When we define the behavior (i.e., the methods bar and baz), we can see that we've specified that the first expected argument is to be the object instance itself. This is because the type uses a form of dynamic dispatch (we learned about this concept back in Chapter 7), and so it needs to know which type to dispatch the behavior to. We'll see this demonstrated in Listing 11-3.

■ **Note**   In Clojure, you don't have to define behavior for every method the protocol defines. This seems to conflict with how other OO-based languages work (e.g., typically when using an interface, you're agreeing to implement its *entire* contract, and so you should define behavior for all the specified methods). That's not the case with Clojure.

Listing 11-3. Calling Our Qux Type (Defined by deftype)

```
(let [b (Qux. "bing bop")]
  (.baz b)
  (.bar b "x")
  (.baz b "y"))

;; user.Qux "bing bop"
;; "hello user.Qux from bar! I've been given: x"
;; "hello user.Qux from baz! I've been given: y"
```

In Listing 11-3, we can see that we've initialized the type (constructor) using the syntax (ClassName. args), which in our example was (Qux. "bing bop"). We then assign the returned object instance to the b let variable, after which we call each subsequent method (including the different arity variations) using the syntax structure of (.methodName objectInstance args), one example being (.bar b "x").

defrecord

A *record* is a data structure very similar to a map in that it's an immutable key/value store, but it's also similar to a struct (where the object it defines has specific fields for allocating to, and so methods can be applied to it).

A key difference to deftype is that defrecord is immutable, whereas deftype can mutate its internal state. But before we discuss *how* to use defrecord, let's first consider some of the reasons *why* you might want to use it.

■ **Note**   If defining methods on a record, then you must also define a protocol (interface).

If you're using dynamic dispatch (e.g., multimethods), then one issue you might come across is that you end up defining similar behavior multiple times when really you're only changing a small part of the overall functionality. The use of defrecord (along with defprotocol) instead allows for the *grouping* of methods and behaviors under a single umbrella type.

From a performance perspective, multimethods are quite slow in comparison to using defrecord, which, as stated previously, is nothing more than an immutable persistent map data structure.

■ **Note**   Internally, records are represented as Java classes.

Listing 11-4. Example of Simple defrecord

```
(defrecord Foo [bar baz qux])
(def f (Foo. "x" "y" "z"))

f ;; #user.Foo{:bar "x", :baz "y", :qux "z"}

(:bar f)
;; "x"
```

So, in Listing 11-4 we can see we've defined a new record called Foo and expect it to have the fields bar, baz, and qux. We then define a new instance of Foo and assign it to the variable f.

What's interesting about this instantiation is the use of the period character (the dot) after the record name. This is one of the ways Clojure can "interop" with Java (remember that "under the covers" the Foo record is actually represented as a Java class).

Once we have our instance created, we're able to access the field by specifying their name followed by the object instance the behavior should be dispatched to for handling (:bar f).

■ **Note**   As the record is really a Java class, we could also access the member field using dot interop notation: (.bar f).

Now, when we defined the record, there were two functions automatically generated for us to utilize. The first is ->Record, and the second is map->Record (where Record is the name of the record). With the former we could create the instance like so, (->Foo "x" "y" "z"), which isn't exactly that much different. I personally prefer the Java interop syntax. But with the latter, you will instantiate the record using a map data structure instead of standard arguments. This can be useful in situations where you already have a data structure that you would like to wrap up inside of a record. For example, (map->Foo {:qux "z" :bar "x" :baz "y"}).

■ **Note**   With map->Record, the keys in the map data structure can be in any order, unlike with Record. or ->Record.

Let's now consider an example where we also would like our record to home a single method called message (as well as the previously defined fields bar, baz, and qux).

Listing 11-5. Example of defrecord with Additional Method

```
(defprotocol IFoo
  (message [obj]))

(defrecord Foo [bar baz qux]
  IFoo
  (message [obj] (str "hello " obj " from " bar ", " baz " and " qux)))

(def f (Foo. "x" "y" "z"))

f
;; #user.Foo{:bar "x", :baz "y", :qux "z"}

(.message f) ;; "hello user.Foo@b679dccc from x, y and z"
```

In Listing 11-5, we can see that because we want to include a method in our record (and because records are really just Java classes) we first need to define a protocol (interface). I've used the convention of prefixing an interface name with a capital i (but you can use whatever convention makes most sense to you). The method we've defined accepts a single parameter, obj.

Next, we define our record the same way as we did previously, but now we have an extra two lines. The first is the interface we wish to support, and the second is the concrete implementation of the protocol. You can also see that the method is able to access the other fields the record has been initialized with.

Lastly, we call our method using dot Java interop dot notation.

Reify

The last item we'll look at is the reify macro, which is able to produce an *anonymous* type. This is unlike both deftype and defrecord, which produce a *named* type. The purpose of reify is solely to provide a way to define a one-time implementation of a pre-existing protocol/record, while its body is a lexical closure, meaning it can access the surrounding local scope.

This is probably best demonstrated by way of an example (see Listing 11-6), which highlights how the reify type is able to access the local scope around it to provide a wrapped response.

■ **Note**   See clojuredocs.org[3] for a more practical example.

Listing 11-6. Example of reify for One-time Anonymous Implementation

```
(defprotocol IFoo (message [obj]))

(defrecord Foo [bar baz qux] IFoo
  (message [obj] (str "hello " obj " from " bar ", " baz " and " qux)))

(def f (Foo. "x" "y" "z"))

(defn wrapper [instance]
  (reify IFoo
    (message [_] (str "wrapped result: " (message instance)))))

(message (wrapper f))
;; "wrapped result: hello user.Foo@b679dccc from x,y and z"
```

Summary

This has been a very short chapter that has focused primarily on a small subset of available object-oriented features within the Clojure language.

We've avoided discussing the Java interop features and how to work with Java code from Clojure, as I feel that this should be a book focused more on Clojure than on Java. The moment you start introducing interop with Java it means requiring some basic knowledge of Java (something outside the scope of this book).

---

[3]https://clojuredocs.org/clojure.core/reify#example-542692cdc026201cdc326d5d

What we've learned is that we can define structure code very well through the use of protocols (defprotocol allows us to define clear interface boundaries), as well as define both mutable and immutable classes using deftype and defrecord. We also saw how we could implement a scoped wrapper for one-off protocol/record implementations.

In the next chapter, we will take a closer look at the Leiningen build tool. So far, we've been using Leiningen as a REPL and simple project tool (for defining some additional dependencies). We'll take a look at the different types of templates and application structures available within Leiningen and at how to produce a quick static web page.

CHAPTER 12

■ ■ ■

Leiningen

In this chapter, I want to talk about the Clojure project-automation tool called Leiningen.[1] Up until this point, we've been exclusively playing around within the REPL environment (thanks to Leiningen's lein repl feature), but we've reached the point now where we should be fairly confident writing Clojure code, and so we need to consider how typical Clojure projects are created, structured, and deployed, and this is where Leiningen really shines.

To demonstrate how Leiningen constructs a project, we'll look at building a simple "Hello World" web application. What this application will do is serve requests for a page that results in an HTML file being returned that displays the message "Hello World." As you can tell, this isn't anything fancy, but it will highlight how easy it is to create a simple static web page just by executing a few quick shell commands.

I'll then proceed to explain how it all works, as well as the various templates available within Leiningen and where to go from that point onward as far as further reading and items of interest.

■ **Note**   This won't be an in-depth discussion on the ins and outs of building complex web applications because, quite frankly, entire books have been written on the subject, and the requirements for every reader will be different.

Ten-second Example

There's no better way to get started than with a super quick, ten-second setup that'll demonstrate the elegance of a few simple commands' resulting in a lot of work and structural setup being automated away from our concern. There are only four commands we need to run, which are as follows:

- `lein new compojure-app foo`

- `cd foo`

- `lein ring server-headless`

- `curl localhost:3000 -i` (or open your browser at http://localhost:3000/)

---

[1]http://leiningen.org/

© Mark McDonnell 2017
M. McDonnell, *Quick Clojure*, DOI 10.1007/978-1-4842-2952-1_12

■ **Note** In Chapter 1, we covered the installation of Leiningen, so please refer back to it if you need to. I'm using macOS, and the following commands shouldn't require any special dependencies to be installed (other than Leiningen itself).

The result of executing these commands can be seen in Listing 12-1. The preceding list of commands could actually end up being one command *shorter* if we wanted by changing the command lein ring server-headless into just lein ring server, which would still start the web server as it did before, but now would *automatically* open a web browser for us and point it to the correct local URL.

If you use the "headless" server version (as just listed), you'll need to open a separate shell in order to execute the curl command, as your current shell will be locked up while the server process is running.

Listing 12-1. Output from Starting Compojure Web Server

```
$ lein new compojure-app foo
Generating a lovely new Compojure project named foo...
$ cd foo
$ lein ring server-headless
foo is starting
2017-06-24 18:21:02.012:INFO:oejs.Server:jetty-7.6.13.v20130916
2017-06-24 18:21:02.072:INFO:oejs.AbstractConnector:Started
SelectChannelConnector@0.0.0.0:3000
Started server on port 3000
```

■ **Note** The syntax structure for the command used in Listing 12-1 is lein new <template> <project-name>. In this simple example, we're using a template called compojure-app. There are many templates available, but this is a popular option for reasons we'll soon discover.

The HTML generated when visiting the Compojure web server (this was the curl command in our previous example) that's started when calling lein ring is shown in Listing 12-2. Ultimately, we see a simple HTML page styled with a static CSS file called screen.css and displaying a central message of "Hello World".

Listing 12-2. HTML Generated

```
HTTP/1.1 200 OK
Date: Sat, 24 Jun 2017 17:41:31 GMT
Content-Type: text/html;charset=UTF-8
Content-Length: 170
Server: Jetty(7.6.13.v20130916)
```

```
<!DOCTYPE html>
<html><head><title>Welcome to foobar</title><link href="/css/screen.css"
rel="stylesheet" type="text/css"></head><body><h1>Hello World!</h1></body>
</html>
```

Help!

Before we take a look at the example Compojure web application in more detail, it's worth mentioning that the Leiningen tool has a very good tutorial and help system built in. For an introductory tutorial (which is definitely worth your time), execute the command shown in Listing 12-3.

Listing 12-3. Leiningen's Built-in Help Tutorial

```
lein tutorial | less
```

■ **Note**   I pipe the tutorial output into the less shell executable because the output from lein tutorial is long and this will save you from having to scroll all the way back up to the beginning.

Any time you're unsure of what a command does, refer to the help command: lein help <command>. So, if (for example) you wanted to know more about the creation of a new Leiningen project, you could run the command lein help new and the output would show you things like what templates are available for you to use, as well as how specific templates are created/resolved.

Compojure

Compojure[2] is a routing library built on top of Ring.[3] If you've not heard of Ring, then I'll quote directly from the Ring GitHub page in order to explain it:

> *Ring is a Clojure web application library inspired by Python's WSGI and Ruby's Rack.*

> —Ring. GitHub

Now, this doesn't necessarily help you if you're equally unfamiliar with WSGI or Rack. In essence, what these two applications share is a standardized interface. So even though they're separate applications (built for two uniquely different languages), it means if you're familiar with one of them, then the other will be recognizable (and understandable) to you as well. Ring supports a similar interface to WSGI and Rack, and this gives developers reassurance that working with Ring should feel natural to them.

---

[2]https://github.com/weavejester/compojure/
[3]https://github.com/ring-clojure/ring

To understand this interface a little better, let's take a look at what a typical "Hello World" HTTP request/response looks like from the point of view of Ruby's Rack (see Listing 12-4).

Listing 12-4. Example of Ruby's Rack Interface

```
[200, { 'Content-Type' => 'text/html' }, ['Hello World!']]
```

What we can see in Listing 12-4 is the relevant Ruby code required to send back a HTTP response. Now, the code syntax isn't something you have to worry too much about, although you will find that the data structures are very familiar, so it should be readable to you at this point.

What we have defined is an array (i.e., vector), and within it are a few basic things required for us to fulfill the interface necessary to send back an HTTP response:

- **Status Code:** 200

- **HTTP Headers:** { 'Content-Type' => 'text/html' }

- **Response Body:** 'Hello World!'

If you look at Listing 12-5, you'll see what this constructed HTTP response would look like from the perspective of a Clojure program. It's almost identical, and so you'll start to see how having a standardized interface can be helpful and useful across languages.

Listing 12-5. Example of HTTP Response in Clojure

```
{:status 200
 :headers {"Content-Type" "text/html"}
 :body "Hello World"}
```

There are more settings we could add to this data structure, but a status code, a set of HTTP headers (for example, you would very likely want to configure things like cache control headers), and a response "body" are all you really need.

■ **Note** Further reading about Ring[4] and Compojure[5] can be found on their respective GitHub Wiki pages.

Compojure Tree Structure

Let's take a quick moment to explore the tree structure of our Compojure web server (see Listing 12-6) that was created using the command lein new compojure-app foo.

---

[4]https://github.com/ring-clojure/ring/wiki
[5]https://github.com/weavejester/compojure/wiki

The structure for a Compojure application isn't too dissimilar to other applications (as we'll see when we view some of the other templates available in Leiningen), but we can see with the Compojure template that we have a src directory that contains all our source code for the web server application.

Alongside the src directory is a test directory that has a set of boilerplate tests included so we can see what a typical test case should look like, as well as a resources directory containing static assets such as JavaScript and CSS style sheets and images.

Listing 12-6. Compojure Tree Structure

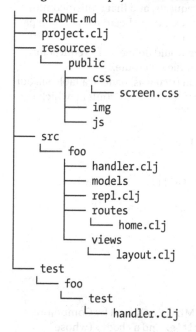

```
├── README.md
├── project.clj
├── resources
│   └── public
│       ├── css
│       │   └── screen.css
│       ├── img
│       └── js
├── src
│   └── foo
│       ├── handler.clj
│       ├── models
│       ├── repl.clj
│       ├── routes
│       │   └── home.clj
│       └── views
│           └── layout.clj
└── test
    └── foo
        └── test
            └── handler.clj
```

In Listing 12-7, we can see how the main home.clj file works. It includes many concepts we've learned in previous chapters, such as namespaces, requiring dependencies and determining how they're referenced, and defining functions responsible for defining the different "routes" our application should handle as well as the "handlers" themselves.

Let's get a quick run-down of home.clj to be sure we understand its setup and what routes our application is automatically configured with (as part of the boilerplate construction).

Listing 12-7. Contents of the Compojure home.clj File

```
(ns foo.routes.home
  (:require [compojure.core :refer :all]
            [foo.views.layout :as layout]))

(defn home []
  (layout/common [:h1 "Hello World!"]))
```

```
(defroutes home-routes
  (GET "/" [] (home)))
```

To start with, we have a namespace defined, and you can see we're pulling in the Compojure core functions, which include the defroutes macro. We also pull in the layout views file from our own tree structure, and that uses the hiccup library for handling constructing an HTML response (see layout.clj in Listing 12-8).

The defroutes macro gives us the ability to define a specific route that our application should handle. By default, our application handles all possible routes by specifying we want our application to handle any GET requests, and that if the incoming path matches "/" (which effectively *all* requests will do, as they all begin with /) then pass that request information to the home function to deal with.

If we wanted to handle the path /foo/bar, then we would define a GET request for "/foo/bar" and then specify which function should handle that route.

The home function calls the layout/common function (that was made available via our views layout.clj file), and we pass that function our response body content, which in this case is an H1 header with the value "Hello World!".

Listing 12-8. Contents of the Compojure layout.clj File

```
(ns foo.views.layout
  (:require [hiccup.page :refer [html5 include-css]]))

(defn common [& body]
  (html5
    [:head
     [:title "Welcome to foo"]
     (include-css "/css/screen.css")]
    [:body body]))
```

We can see from Listing 12-8 what the default HTML is that's used by Compojure. It's a simple HTML page consisting of a <head> and <title> and a <body> (whose contents are provided by the caller of the common function). We can also see it includes a screen.css file, which is what gives our page its default styling.

Tests

Compojure also constructs some basic tests for us in the test/foo/test/handler.clj file (see Listing 12-9). This file utilizes the built-in Clojure testing library clojure.test[6] in order to define some simple tests that verify the web server is running as expected.

---

[6]https://clojure.github.io/clojure/clojure.test-api.html

■ **Note**   These tests are integration tests rather than unit tests. In short, a *unit test* is for verifying the behavior of an individual function (or unit of code), whereas an *integration test* verifies the system as a whole is working as expected. For more information on the difference, I refer you to a short but good explanation by Nathan Hughes.[7]

Listing 12-9. Contents of Compojure's `test/handler.clj` File

```
(ns foo.test.handler
  (:use clojure.test
        ring.mock.request
        foo.handler))

(deftest test-app
  (testing "main route"
    (let [response (app (request :get "/"))]
      (is (= (:status response) 200))
      (is (.contains (:body response) "Hello World"))))

  (testing "not-found route"
    (let [response (app (request :get "/invalid"))]
      (is (= (:status response) 404)))))
```

In Listing 12-9, we can see that we're pulling in the `clojure.test` dependency along with a dependency specified by Ring itself, which is its mock request library.[8] We also pull in the Compojure handler file, as that gives us access to the app function within that file.

From the code, we can see that we're now able to provide a fake (i.e., mocked) request object into the app function, and subsequently we can inspect the response and identify if the relevant details came back as we had expected them to.

As far as Listing 12-9 is concerned, we can see that we're expecting that a request to `"/"` will result in the response contents `"Hello World"`, and that the response status code will be a 200 code (which indicates a successful request).

The second test validates that the web server returns the status code 404 when a request is received by the web server for a path that it isn't configured to handle (so, in this case, a request to the nonsensical path `"/invalid"` was made).

In order to run these tests, we need to utilize a sub-command of Leiningen: `lein test`. This command will locate all the tests within the test directory and execute them one by one. We can also execute only specific test suites by specifying the relevant namespace. For example, `lein test :only foo.test.handler/test-app`.

---

[7]https://stackoverflow.com/a/5357837/4288305
[8]https://github.com/ring-clojure/ring-mock

> ■ **Note**   test-app is the containing suite of tests defined in tests/handler.clj, and within that we have a set of testing "contexts" that allow us to display specific output messages.

If all is well, you'll see the output shown in Listing 12-10; otherwise, if there's an error (let's say we changed the expected status code output for a successful request to be 202 instead of 200) you'll see what's shown in Listing 12-11.

Listing 12-10. Successful Test Output

```
lein test foo.test.handler

Ran 1 tests containing 3 assertions.
0 failures, 0 errors.
```

Listing 12-11. Failed Test Output

```
lein test foo.test.handler

lein test :only foo.test.handler/test-app

FAIL in (test-app) (handler.clj:9)
main route
expected: (= (:status response) 202)
  actual: (not (= 200 202))

Ran 1 tests containing 3 assertions.
1 failures, 0 errors.
Tests failed.
```

That covers things as far as the basic setup and usage of a Compojure web application are concerned. There's obviously lots more to what Compojure can do and how it can be configured, but, as mentioned earlier, there are entire books based on the topic of Clojure web development, so let's instead now turn our attention to the set of templates that are included as part of Leiningen, as this will show us what other types of applications we can build.

Templates

One thing you will notice as we review the various templates that are built-in with Leiningen (there are *many* other templates that can be found on the Internet for all types of requirements) is that the tree structure isn't vastly different between each template, and this is both a good thing (as it provides a consistent base to work from) and a bad thing (as it makes it hard to distinguish the differences and use cases).

So, to recap what we know so far: Leiningen uses the concept of templates to dynamically construct a new project. There are a few built-in templates, and there are numerous external templates (such as the Compojure template I used in the ten-second example). There are (at the time of writing) four separate built-in templates available, as follows:

- **template**: a meta-template for 'lein new' templates
- **default**: a general project template for libraries
- **app**: an application project template
- **plugin**: a Leiningen plugin project template

template

So, the first template in the list is actually a template used to define *new* templates. I'm not going to cover how to create your own templates, as it's outside the scope of this book, and to be honest I've also never had a need to use them myself, as nearly every possible use case I've had has already been covered by the open source community. See Listing 12-12.

Listing 12-12. Tree Structure for the Leiningen "template" Template

```
├── CHANGELOG.md
├── LICENSE
├── README.md
├── project.clj
├── resources
│   └── leiningen
│       └── new
│           └── foo
│               └── foo.clj
└── src
    └── leiningen
        └── new
            └── foo.clj
```

That being said, you might have some organizational structures and dependencies that you have to use for all your work-related projects, and so maybe creating a template for simplifying and quickening that tedious process over and over would be beneficial.

■ **Note** An example of an organization's using its own templates is the ClojureWerks lein-template repository.[9]

---

[9]https://github.com/clojurewerkz/lein-template

In Listing 12-12, we can see what the directory structure for a template application looks like. This is just so we have a frame of reference compared to the other templates (see Listing 12-12). Here's a quick reminder of the command required to create this project: `lein new template <name>`.

■ **Note**   Leiningen provides a great/short official document that explains the relevant steps for creating your own template.[10]

In essence, in order to use a new template project, you would need to deploy your template to Clojars[11] (which is Clojure's open/public repository of community-driven libraries). If you named the repo something like `<name>/lein-template` (where `<name>` is whatever you want your template to be referred to as), then a Clojure developer could execute `lein new <name> <project_name>`, and this would cause Leiningen to search Clojars for a template project under the title `<name>/lein-template`.

default

The second template (as the description stated earlier) is used for general-purpose libraries rather than for an actual application. Let's take a look at its directory structure (see Listing 12-13).

Listing 12-13. Tree Structure for the Leiningen "default" Template

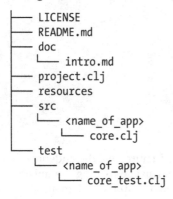

```
├── LICENSE
├── README.md
├── doc
│   └── intro.md
├── project.clj
├── resources
├── src
│   └── <name_of_app>
│       └── core.clj
└── test
    └── <name_of_app>
        └── core_test.clj
```

There are two ways you can generate a default project. You can be either explicit or implicit. If we're being *explicit*, then we're specifying the template name: `lein new default <name>`. You can also be *implicit* by leaving off the "default" part.

---

[10]https://github.com/technomancy/leiningen/blob/master/doc/TEMPLATES.md
[11]https://clojars.org/

■ **Note** As long as there isn't a template called <name>, then Leiningen will presume that what you specify is the project name for the default template.

What we can see in Listing 12-13 is that it's very lean. If we look at project.clj we can see there are no dependencies other than Clojure itself, and that the core.clj is equally light in that it has a single function inside it. The function defined in core.clj is named after the project, and it simply prints "Hello World" to the stdout (i.e., the terminal screen).

Interestingly, you'll see that project.clj doesn't define a entrypoint (like we saw with the Compojure template's project.clj). This helps to enforce the concept that this code base doesn't need one, as it is expected to be loaded within another code base as a dependency library, and so it will be required via the ns macro.

app

The third template type is "app," and although its directory structure (see Listing 12-14) is the same as the library template, its purpose is simply to execute some general-purpose code.

What do we mean by *general purpose*? Well, you could create a command-line application, or maybe you decide to download the relevant dependencies for building a web application (and that will become your project focus). This is fundamentally different from the library template whose purpose is for the code to be loaded *within* another project/application as a dependency/library.

Listing 12-14. Tree Structure for the Leiningen "app" Template

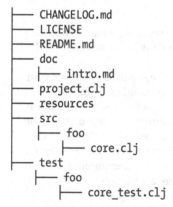

```
├── CHANGELOG.md
├── LICENSE
├── README.md
├── doc
│   ├── intro.md
├── project.clj
├── resources
├── src
│   ├── foo
│       ├── core.clj
├── test
    ├── foo
        ├── core_test.clj
```

With this difference in mind, if you were to now look at the contents of the core.clj file within the src directory, you would see that its contents are slightly different than the library template's core.clj in that they define a main function (prefixed with a hyphen: defn -main). Also, at the top of that file you'll see that the namespace macro has included an extra configuration setting of (:gen-class). Lastly, the project.clj file itself has a :main attribute that points to our core.clj file to indicate this is the file that should be executed when the lein run command is executed.

Let's now briefly review these three differences (:main, -main, and gen-class) to be sure we understand their purposes. The :main attribute's purpose is to notify Leiningen of the entrypoint to your application, but you'll likely have noticed there was an extra attribute defined: ^:skip-aot. What this does is skip Clojure's "Ahead-of-Time" (AOT) compilation step,[12] which can be useful for speeding up your application's startup by compiling the code into JVM bytecode.

Considering AOT compilation can help performance, why might we want to skip it? Well, in some cases your code might rely on input that you'll only know at runtime, and so if your code references an environment variable (for example) that is not available at the point in time of compilation (let's say it's only available on the server where the application is deployed), then this would mean the compilation would change the code to use the value nil for that environment variable wherever it's referenced in the code.

■ **Note** There are ways to solve these types of issues, but they're outside the scope/focus of this book.

The references to (gen-class) and the function -main are used together as they're intrinsically coupled. The gen-class tells Clojure's compiler to create a new Java class for your namespace, while -main defines the behavior of that Java class.

Finally, this all ties back in with the use of the :main attribute in the project.clj, as it indicates there is a Java class that should be used as the entrypoint for the application. I suggest reading the reference material[13] to learn more about these features.

plugin

The fourth template type is "plugin," and this is useful for developing plugin[14] code for your Clojure applications. An example of what a plugin can do is lein-eastwood,[15] which is a Clojure code linting tool.

In order to use a plugin (such as lein-eastwood) you'll be required to update your project.clj file to reference the plugin (for example, adding :plugins [[jonase/eastwood "0.2.4"]]). Once you do that you'll find the plugin is now made available as a subcommand of Leiningen and can execute code in the context of your project. In the case of lein-eastwood, it is able to review (i.e. lint) your code for common mistakes.

Listing 12-15 shows a typical directory structure for a Leiningen plugin. To help give you an idea of what other type of behaviors plugins can offer, I recommend you sift through the official list[16] of Leiningen plugins (of which there are many!).

---

[12]https://clojure.org/reference/compilation
[13]https://clojure.org/reference/compilation
[14]https://github.com/technomancy/leiningen/blob/master/doc/PLUGINS.md
[15]https://github.com/jonase/eastwood
[16]https://github.com/technomancy/leiningen/wiki/Plugins

Listing 12-15. Tree Structure for the Leiningen "plugin" Template

```
├── LICENSE
├── README.md
├── project.clj
├── src
    ├── leiningen
        ├── <name_of_plugin>.clj
```

■ **Note**   Leiningen provides a good document on how to create your own plugins[17] that is highly recommended.

Project File

One consistent item found across all these different projects/template types is the project file itself: project.clj. The main purpose of this file is to bootstrap your application. It does this by defining your project's dependencies and pulling them down for you when you first run your project's application code.

The project.clj also allows you to associate metadata, such as a project description and URL, as well as define any plugins you wish to use (and many more things).

For a complete list of configuration settings available, I would suggest reading through the Leiningen template example file,[18] which explains every single setting available in great detail (and there are lots of them).

Let's take a look at the project.clj file for a generic Compojure "Hello World" application (like the one we created earlier) and see if we can get a better understanding of the different aspects of the configuration we've been given.

Listing 12-16. Compojure project.clj File

```
(defproject compojure-foo "0.1.0-SNAPSHOT"
  :description "FIXME: write description"
  :url "http://example.com/FIXME"
  :dependencies [[org.clojure/clojure "1.8.0"]
                 [compojure "1.5.2"]
                 [hiccup "1.0.5"]
                 [ring-server "0.4.0"]]
  :plugins [[lein-ring "0.8.12"]]
  :ring {:handler compojure-foo.handler/app
         :init compojure-foo.handler/init
         :destroy compojure-foo.handler/destroy}
  :profiles
```

---

[17]https://github.com/technomancy/leiningen/blob/master/doc/PLUGINS.md
[18]https://github.com/technomancy/leiningen/blob/master/sample.project.clj

```
{:uberjar {:aot :all}
 :production
 {:ring
  {:open-browser? false, :stacktraces? false, :auto-reload? false}}
 :dev
 {:dependencies [[ring-mock "0.1.5"] [ring/ring-devel "1.5.1"]]}})
```

In Listing 12-16, we can see we have some Clojure code that uses the defproject macro to construct the project's bootstrap. It's already set up with the name we provided when running lein new..., and it has defaulted the version of the application to 0.1.0-SNAPSHOT. We can change this to any value we want when we come to release our application (e.g., you might want to change it to 1.0.0 or 0.0.1).

■ **Note** Typically, the version format used here would suggest semantic versioning[19]: <Major>.<Minor>.<Patch> while the use of SNAPSHOT is a Java version-naming convention.

From there we have a standard :description field and an associated :url field so users know where the source code (or promotional branding) for the project can be located.

We also have a :dependencies field (arguably one of the most important items in this file). For the Compojure application, we find the Compojure app template has automatically pre-filled in some useful dependencies for us:

- org.clojure/clojure "1.8.0" — the Clojure language

- compojure "1.5.2" — HTTP request routing library[20]

- hiccup "1.0.5" — a library for rendering HTML[21]

- ring-server "0.4.0" — web server for Ring interface[22]

■ **Note** When you run Leiningen it will automatically pull down all your dependencies, but you can also do this manually at any point using the sub-command lein deps.

Moving on, we have the :plugins setting, which has pulled in the plugin lein-ring[23] and which is responsible for automating some common Ring-based tasks. This plugin adds an additional setting to the project.clj file and once specified we're required to include the following attribute: :ring {...configuration...}.

---

[19]http://semver.org/
[20]https://github.com/weavejester/compojure
[21]https://github.com/weavejester/hiccup
[22]https://github.com/weavejester/ring-server
[23]https://github.com/weavejester/lein-ring

As we can see from the project.clj file itself, when the Compojure template is used it pre-fills the :ring attribute configuration automatically for us so that it knows where the main handler function can be located, as well as identifies functions for set-up and tear-down behaviors (which are no-op functions by default, meaning they are defined functions, but don't have any behaviors defined).

Following on from there, we see the :profiles setting. This allows us to define certain behavior dependent on the environment. So we can see there is a :productions attribute that defines how the application should behave in a production setting (e.g., we set :auto-reload? false as that type of behavior is only useful when developing your application code locally, and we also set :stacktraces? false as we want to hide that type of information from our users). Similarly, we have a :dev attribute where we specify dependencies that are only useful when developing locally.

If you would like to learn more about these configuration options, then I'd advise you to review the lein-ring plugin's GitHub page,[24] which will be up-to-date with the latest details.

■ **Note**   You can test your profiles locally by running your application using the with-profile option (e.g., lein with-profile production run some_app).

---

compojure vs. compojure-app

We created a "Hello World" example using lein new compojure-app <name_of_app>, and this provided us with lots of stuff for free, such as the handling of static assets and the serving up of some basic CSS to go along with our HTTP response.

But we could have also used lein new compojure <name_of_app> (notice compojure-app is now just compojure), which would still provide us a simple web service like it did before, but now it is stripped back even further! This means no fancy HTML wrapped around our "Hello World" message, just plain text sent back to the browser.

I recommend exploring the other differences between the two template types, but which template you choose ultimately depends on how comfortable you are setting up a lot of the tedious aspects of handling rich HTML responses. For most people, compojure-app is the simplest route to get up and running quickly and efficiently.

Real-World Library Example

Sometimes it's best to consider what a *real* project looks like. For example, building a Clojure web application is one thing (most devs can muddle along with that—maybe with some Google assistance thrown in), but I found from my own personal experience that building a library that is *consumed* by another application can be quite a confusing process. So, I wanted to show you a small Clojure library I wrote to help me use a tool called Spurious[25] (this is an example from a few years ago, but the principle still stands).

---

[24]https://github.com/weavejester/lein-ring#web-server-options
[25]https://github.com/spurious-io/spurious

We'll start by understanding what Spurious is, and then we'll take a look through the library project I created, as well as look briefly over an example application that consumed the library. But first, let's refer to the Spurious README to see how it describes itself:

> *Spurious is a toolset allowing development against a subset of AWS[26] resources, locally. The services are run as Docker containers, and Spurious manages their lifecycle and linking so all you have to worry about is using the services. To use Spurious, you'll need to change the endpoint and port for each AWS service to those provided by Spurious.*

—Spurious. GitHub

In a nutshell, Spurious attempts to save you money while developing applications that use AWS services (by running those services locally). This is awesome for me because I use AWS a lot, and it allows me to experiment without having to pay for the pleasure of playing around with some code that might never become anything.

■ **Note** To make things more complicated (for myself) I needed my library code to work when loaded both within a standard Clojure application as well as when the application was run from within a Docker container (which didn't necessarily result in more code, but added more complexity to the overall process and understanding of how to write and test my library).

You can find my library code online, hosted with GitHub,[27] as well as the example application that consumes the library.[28] I won't be covering the ins and outs of either, but I link to them, as they'll make for a useful reference point.

Consumer

Let's start with the example application and how it consumes my library. If you look at the `project.clj` you'll see that I've simply defined my library as being a dependency. Take a look at Listing 12-17 for a stripped-back example.

Listing 12-17. Example of Consumer `project.clj`

```
(defproject spurious-clojure-example "0.1.0"
  :dependencies [[spurious-aws-sdk-helper "0.2.0"]])
```

So, nothing special here; we have a dependency and we're indicating the specific version we wish our application to use.

---

[26]http://aws.amazon.com/
[27]https://github.com/integralist/spurious-clojure-aws-sdk-helper
[28]https://github.com/integralist/spurious-clojure-example

Local Testing

In case you're unfamiliar with the process of releasing a library, I'll quickly detour into what I needed to do in order to be able to test and load my own library as a dependency.

First, I needed to deploy my library to Clojure's online repository of available libraries (called Clojars[29]). This requires you to follow the instructions provided by Leiningen,[30] but in essence the steps involved are to register for an account and then execute the sub-command `lein deploy clojars`.

But how do you go about testing your library code *before* releasing it (how do you know it'll work)? You don't want to push up version 1.0.0 and then go to use it and find there was a bug you didn't expect. You want to test the library locally using a local application so you can be 100 percent sure it works (this was especially important to me, as my library needed to work within a Docker container, and I just wasn't confident that I could verify that without manual steps).

The solution to that problem was simply to install the library to my local cache directory. To understand what this means, you need to realize that Leiningen creates a local cache of your dependencies. It does this so it doesn't have to keep downloading the same dependency over and over for every project you create.

This means we can take advantage of the local cache to trick Leiningen into thinking it has already downloaded the dependency from online (i.e., downloaded it from Clojars), even if the dependency doesn't yet exist online. To do that you simply run (from inside your library project directory) `lein install`, and this will install your library into your local `~/.m2` cache directory.

Loading the Dependency

Take a look at Listing 12-18 to see what the consumer's `home.clj` file looks like. Here, you'll see how we're pulling the library for consumption.

Listing 12-18. Load the External Dependency (Shortened for Brevity)

```
(ns spurious-clojure-example.routes.home
  (:require [compojure.core :refer :all]
            [spurious-aws-sdk-helper.core :as core]
            [spurious-aws-sdk-helper.utils :refer [endpoint cred]]))
```

You can see I'm pulling in the `core` namespace and renaming it so it makes it easier for me to reference the public functions contained within that loaded namespace (e.g., `core/configure`). You can also see I refer in two functions from my `utils` namespace: `endpoint` and `cred`.

Without getting bogged down in a line-by-line explanation, that's generally all there is to loading the library within the consumer. This tallies up with everything we've learned so far about namespaces and Leiningen projects.

---

[29]https://clojars.org/
[30]https://github.com/technomancy/leiningen/blob/stable/doc/TUTORIAL.md

Reviewing the Library

When looking at our helper library, we can see that I've used an extremely simple and *flat* folder structure (Listing 12-19). It shows that your hierarchy doesn't have to be deep and nested if you don't need it to be.

Listing 12-19. Clojure Library Simple Tree Structure

```
.
├── src
│   ├── spurious_aws_sdk_helper
│   │   ├── core.clj
│   │   ├── dynamodb.clj
│   │   ├── s3.clj
│   │   ├── sqs.clj
│   │   ├── utils.clj
├── project.clj
```

I have a single `src` folder, and inside that I have a single folder called `spurious_aws_sdk_helper`, which contains all the Clojure files required by my library. The `core.clj` is responsible for loading the remaining files: `dynamodb.clj`, `s3.clj`, and `sqs.clj`.

The `utils.clj` file contains (as you would expect) lots of utility functions. Only two functions in this file are public and exposed as such so that our consuming application can call them to get the service set up and running; the rest of the functions are all private and used internally by the library itself.

■ **Note**   Remember, you can tell when a function is defined as private by the use of the hyphen `defn-` (public functions use the standard `defn` macro that you're already familiar with).

One item of interest is how the `configure` function with the `core` namespace is using a multi-arity function in order to execute different behaviors depending on whether an `opts` map was provided or not.

Listing 12-20. Example of a Simple Multi-arity Function

```
(defn configure
  ([type]
   (s3/setup  type)
   (ddb/setup type))
  ([type opts]
   (if-let [name   (:s3  opts)] (s3/setup  type name))
   (if-let [name   (:sqs opts)] (sqs/setup type name))
   (if-let [schema (:ddb opts)]
     (ddb/setup type (yaml/parse-string schema)))))
```

As you can see from Listing 12-20, if no opts is provided then we just call the setup method for both S3 and DynamoDB; otherwise, if an opts argument is provided then we use if-let to extract the relevant key (e.g., :s3, :sqs, or :ddb) from the opts hash provided, and then associate it with the name symbol. We again will call the setup method for each service, and this time we pass in name.

■ **Note**   We've not seen if-let before, but it's an immensely useful macro that lets us execute a block of code only if the let binding is able to destruct the data into the specified symbol successfully (you also have similar options, such as when-let and letfn, which are worth exploring further).

Preparing for Deploy

At this point, let's assume you have a project you want to deploy (if it's a library, then as I mentioned earlier you'll need to deploy the library to Clojars, where it can then be consumed by other applications).

Otherwise, if this is a standard application and not a library, then Leiningen also provides a single command to help us package our application in such a way that it can be easily deployed to a production server and run with relatively little fuss: lein uberjar.

The uberjar command, when configured properly from within your project.clj (I'll cover that in a moment), will generate a single jar file that contains your project code as well as all its dependencies. If you've not dealt with the .jar format before, Listing 12-21 will show you how you can execute a jar from the command line.

Listing 12-21. Example of How to Execute a Jar via the Terminal

```
java -jar my_jar_file.jar <your> <args> <here>
```

If you use the lein-tar plugin,[31] then you'll have at your disposal the lein tar command, and if you're using lein-ring,[32] then you can build a web application using lein ring uberjar (or lein ring war for older servers, if you require that).

Now, coming back to the standard lein uberjar command, I mentioned earlier that you need to configure your application in order for that command to work properly. You'll need to modify your project.clj to include a :main key and assign a namespace that points to the entry point of your application.

If you look at the example application,[33] you'll see I set the namespace to :main ^:skip-aot spurious-clojure-example.repl. The namespace points to src/spurious_clojure_example/repl.clj, and inside that file I've added a new function called main. The main function is what should start up the web server (see Listing 12-22).

---

[31]https://github.com/technomancy/lein-tar
[32]https://github.com/weavejester/lein-ring
[33]https://github.com/integralist/spurious-clojure-example/

Listing 12-22. Example main Function in Clojure Example App

```
(defn -main []
  (start-server))
```

■ **Note** As we mentioned earlier, our main entry point also needs (gen-class), so you'll notice I've included that in the file as well.

Effectively, what it all boils down to is (depending on what your application does): modify the :main key in your project.clj to point to a file that has a main function that bootstraps your application in whatever way it needs to, and make sure to add (gen-class) to the top of the file (see earlier in the chapter to understand why).

Summary

By the end of this chapter, we have gained a good understanding of the basics of using Leiningen and constructing a project using specific templates (such as compojure-app) as well as the differences between the various built-in templates.

I've not delved too deeply into building web applications because the requirements are too vast and unique for each project. If you're interested in the topic of web development with Clojure, then I would strongly suggest reading *Web Development with Clojure*.[34] It's a great introduction to the sheer wealth of Clojure libraries and plugins that can be composed together to build a robust web-based application.

In the next chapter, we'll be looking at how to build a command-line interface application. It'll cover the basics of the setup and the various tools available for developing this kind of application. This should help you to expand your vision of Clojure beyond just a web-based programming language and open up new possibilities for useful business tools that can take advantage of your operating system.

---

[34]https://pragprog.com/book/dswdcloj/web-development-with-clojure

■ ■ ■

CHAPTER 13

Command-Line Applications

In this chapter, we're going to do two things: first, we're going to review Clojure's `tools.cli` library in order to understand how we can utilize it to help us design and develop command-line applications. Second, we'll look at how to package up this application in order for us to be able to distribute it.

Building command-line applications is something that most developers enjoy doing because it exposes a way to enrich their working environment (as well as the environment of their team or wider dev community if they're designing a tool that is abstract enough to be useful to more than just themselves). The possibilities are endless when designing a CLI tool, as you have so much scope to work with.

Once we've reviewed `clojure/tools.cli` and the packaging options, you'll find that we'll have covered the vast majority of what you need to know. The rest is up to you; how you design and structure the application will depend on the tool you're looking to build and the problem you're trying to solve.

Let's begin by first creating a fresh project using the Leiningen app template, which we saw in the previous chapter. The command is `lein new app cli-foo` (you can name your application whatever you like, but I've gone with the simple but effective `cli-foo`).

Inside of that project, open your `project.clj` and update the dependencies key to include the `clojure/tools.cli` dependency. See Listing 13-1 to view the change in context.

Listing 13-1. Update `project.clj` to Include `tools.cli` Dependency

```
(defproject cli-foo "0.1.0-SNAPSHOT"
  :description "FIXME: write description"
  :url "http://example.com/FIXME"
  :license {:name "Eclipse Public License"
            :url "http://www.eclipse.org/legal/epl-v10.html"}
  :dependencies [[org.clojure/clojure "1.8.0"]
                 [org.clojure/tools.cli "0.3.5"]]
  :main ^:skip-aot cli-foo.core
  :target-path "target/%s"
  :profiles {:uberjar {:aot :all}})
```

© Mark McDonnell 2017
M. McDonnell, *Quick Clojure*, DOI 10.1007/978-1-4842-2952-1_13

■ **Note**   One thing you'll want to do (and we'll explain why later) is to delete the :target-path attribute from the project.clj.

OK. Let's now open up src/cli_foo/core.clj and make the modifications seen in Listing 13-2. There's a lot going on, so we'll take some time to break down each change to be sure we understand what it is we're doing and why.

The first thing you'll notice is that we update the ns macro to ensure we're pulling in the parse-opts function from the cli namespace. This allows us to parse the incoming arguments (provided by the user when using the tool) and to intelligently handle the input in a way that makes sense for our application.

Listing 13-2. The Main Application Logic for Our Command-Line Tool

```
(ns cli-foo.core
  (:require [clojure.tools.cli :refer [parse-opts]])
  (:gen-class))

(defn exit [status msg]
  (println msg)
  (System/exit status))

(def cli-options
  [["-p" "--port PORT" "Port number"
    :default 80
    :parse-fn #(Integer/parseInt %)
    :validate [#(< 0 % 0x10000) "Must be a number between 0 and 65536"]]
   ["-v" nil "Verbosity level"
    :id :verbosity
    :default 0
    :assoc-fn (fn [opts k v] (update-in opts [k] inc))]
   ["-x" "--xxx WHATEVER", "A description for this option"
    :default 123]
   ["-h" "--help"
    :id :custom-help]])

(defn -main [& args]
  (let [{:keys [options arguments errors summary]} (parse-opts args
    cli-options)]
    (cond
      (:custom-help options) (exit 0 summary)
      (not (nil? errors)) (exit 1 errors)
      :else (exit 0 (parse-opts args cli-options)))))
```

The next thing you'll notice is that we define an exit function. The purpose of this function is to accept an "exit code" (this would typically be 0 if everything were executed successfully, or a positive number if there were an error[1]). We pass the exit code to the System/exit function, which will ensure the application shuts down appropriately and correctly. The function also accepts a msg argument, which as you can imagine will be used for printing a message. The message is sent to stdout (standard out[2]), which in this case is the terminal screen.

After that, we define a cli-options variable and have assigned to it a large nested vector data structure with a very specific set of attributes defined. Each item in the vector defines an individual *flag*.

■ **Note** A *flag* is what we provide to a command-line application in order to configure its behavior. For example, ls -l -a is the ls command (this lists all files and directories) with two flags -l and -a applied, which affects the displayed output.

We can see that we have the following flags defined (these are all arbitrarily made up flags), and we'll soon see that we don't actually do very much with these flags in the application itself other than print them to the screen, but they've been chosen to demonstrate some different aspects of the tools.cli library:

- -p, --port: demonstrates :parse-fn and :validate

- -v, --verbosity: demonstrates :assoc-fn

- -x, --xxx: demonstrates :default

- -h, --help: demonstrates :id

■ **Note** To see the full list of attributes available, I recommend you read through the source code file, which documents them all.[3]

We'll come back to what the flags mean and how they work, but let's move on to the final segment of the code, which is the -main function. The first thing we do in this function is call the parse-opts function and provide it with the arguments that were given to us via the user of the command-line tool, along with the cli-options flags we defined and configured.

What we get back from parse-opts is a map data structure consisting of four keys: :options, :arguments, :summary, and :errors. See Listing 13-3 for the description assigned to each of them. We assign each key to a specific symbol for easy referencing.

---

[1]http://tldp.org/LDP/abs/html/exitcodes.html
[2]https://en.wikipedia.org/wiki/Standard_streams
[3]https://github.com/clojure/tools.cli/blob/master/src/main/clojure/cljs/tools/cli.cljs

Listing 13-3. Map Returned from `parse-opts` Function

```
{:options    Options map, keyed by :id, mapped to the parsed value
 :arguments  A vector of unprocessed arguments
 :summary    A string containing a minimal options summary
 :errors     A possible vector of error message strings}
```

Next, within the `-main` function we define a condition that says that if the user has included the flag `-h` or `--help`, then we should call the `exit` function and pass it the `:summary` value returned by `parse-opts`.

You'll also notice that we're identifying whether the help flag was specified by looking up the `:id` we defined for that flag (`:custom-help`) in the `:options` field that was returned by `parse-opts`.

Next, after that condition we state that if there was an error parsing the arguments and/or flags, then we should call the `exit` function but provide the exit code 1 (which indicates an error) and then pass the error message itself that was returned by `parse-opts` (specifically, this is the `:errors` field) so the user can see what they might have done wrong.

Finally, we have an `else` statement that says to call the `exit` function and provide it the exit code 0 (which indicates all is well) and simply call `parse-opts` again and use its return value as the thing we're going to display to the user.

At this point, we know enough about this application to start looking at how to compile and run it. We'll do this next, and then after we've run the application and explored how we interact with it, we can go back and review the flag configuration settings we defined and assigned to the `cli-options` variable, hopefully with a stronger understanding of how they're used in practice.

Running the cli Application

There are three ways we could potentially run this application right now:

1. Directly via Leiningen

2. Compiling the application into a jar

3. Compiling the application into a binary

While we're just testing things, we'll use option 1. Later, I'll show you options 2 and 3, although really option 3 is the one you'll most likely be interested in, as that is the option that will allow us to run the application like a true command-line binary (much like the standard binaries you already use, such as `ls` or `cat`, etc.).

Running via Leiningen

To run the command-line application via Leiningen, we simply execute a command with the following syntax structure: `lein run <options> <arguments>`. For example, in Listing 13-4 we can see one such example that would work for the application we've defined.

Listing 13-4. Executing Our Command-Line Application

```
lein run -v -p 9090 -x 666 arg1 arg2 arg3
```

The output of the preceding command can be seen in Listing 13-5, and, as we can see, the displayed output is what we would expect to see return from the parse-opts function.

Listing 13-5. Output from Our Application

```
{:options {:xxx 666, :verbosity 1, :port 9090}, :arguments [arg1 arg2 arg3],
:summary    -p, --port PORT      80   Port number
  -v                              Verbosity level
  -x, --xxx WHATEVER   123  A description for this option
  -h, --help, :errors nil}
```

Remember in Listing 13-3 how we described the four attributes that were expected to be included in the returned map data structure? Well, we can see them here and what their actual values have been assigned. This will help us better understand how to utilize them in our app.

■ **Note**   If there were no errors, then the :errors field is expected to be assigned the nil value.

Running via a Jar

Running the application from a jar isn't that much different from running it directly via Leiningen. The flag options and arguments are no different; it's just you have to reference a jar file instead of referring to Leiningen.

This means we need to first compile the app into a jar, which you would do using the command lein uberjar. Once you run that command, you should see output similar to that in Listing 13-6.

Listing 13-6. Output of Generating a Jar of Your Application

```
Compiling cli-foo.core
Created /Users/M/cli-foo/target/uberjar+uberjar/cli-foo-0.1.0-SNAPSHOT.jar
Created /Users/M/cli-foo/target/uberjar/cli-foo-0.1.0-SNAPSHOT-standalone.
jar
```

You can see from this output that the command has generated a set of jars for us to use (and deploy, if this were indeed a standard application rather than a command-line variety). Let's now see how we run the generated jar file. Assuming you're currently inside the cli-foo directory, you should execute the command seen in Listing 13-7.

Listing 13-7. Jar Command to Run Our Application

```
java -jar target/cli-foo-0.1.0-SNAPSHOT-standalone.jar -v -p 9090 -x 666
arg1 arg2 arg3
```

Running via Binary

This is the packaging option that I believe will be of most interest to readers. We would like our application to be run from any operating system (OS) with minimal setup and hassle. To do that we'll need to utilize an external plugin.

The plugin we'll be using is called lein-bin,[4] and it takes the uberjar Leiningen would otherwise produce and wraps it in another format along with a specific configuration to allow it to be run from Windows, Mac, or Linux environments.

To start, we need to update the project.clj with the lein-bin plugin, as well as provide some additional settings, such as giving our binary a name (in this case, I want my binary to be integralist). We'll also configure the binary to be added to the local user bin path so I can run it implicitly with the format: integralist <options> <arguments>.

■ **Note** The bin path is where most of your OS' executable binaries are stored. There's a system directory for binaries, /usr/bin, and there's a user directory at /usr/local/ bin. We'll want to stick our binary in the user-specific directory, because that is where any binaries installed by a user should go.

In Listing 13-8, you'll see the required changes in context of the full project.clj file. We've added the :plugin attribute (as this is our first plugin for this project), and we've added the new plugin-specific attribute :bin, which we set up so that it names our executable integralist, and it will also copy the generated executable into our /usr/ local/bin directory automatically for us.

Listing 13-8. Configure lein-bin via the project.clj File

```
(defproject cli-foo "0.1.0-SNAPSHOT"
  :description "FIXME: write description"
  :url "http://example.com/FIXME"
  :license {:name "Eclipse Public License"
            :url "http://www.eclipse.org/legal/epl-v10.html"}
  :dependencies [[org.clojure/clojure "1.8.0"]
                 [org.clojure/tools.cli "0.3.5"]]
  :plugins [[lein-bin "0.3.4"]]
  :bin {:name "integralist"
        :bin-path "/usr/local/bin"}
  :main ^:skip-aot cli-foo.core
  :profiles {:uberjar {:aot :all}})
```

---

[4]https://github.com/raynes/lein-bin

If you run `lein repl` now, you should find that Leiningen will download the newly defined plugin. The output will look like Listing 13-9 and highlights some nested dependencies required.

Listing 13-9. Pulling Down the `lein-bin` Plugin and Its Dependencies

```
Retrieving lein-bin/lein-bin/0.3.4/lein-bin-0.3.4.pom from clojars
Retrieving me/raynes/fs/1.4.0/fs-1.4.0.pom from clojars
Retrieving org/apache/commons/commons-compress/1.3/commons-compress-1.3.pom
from central
Retrieving org/apache/commons/commons-compress/1.3/commons-compress-1.3.jar
from central
Retrieving lein-bin/lein-bin/0.3.4/lein-bin-0.3.4.jar from clojars
Retrieving me/raynes/fs/1.4.0/fs-1.4.0.jar from clojars
```

At this point, you'll have a `lein bin` command available to you. If you execute that command from the project directory, you'll see output similar to that shown in Listing 13-10. With the binary now compiled and it's being copied into your `/usr/local/bin` directory, you'll find it should be available to you from anywhere on your computer.

■ **Note**   This is because your `$PATH` environment variable is pre-configured to look up executables in the `/usr/local/bin` directory.

Listing 13-10. Output from `lein-bin` Command

```
Compiling cli-foo.core
Created /Users/M/code/clojure/cli-foo/target/cli-foo-0.1.0-SNAPSHOT.jar
Created /Users/M/code/clojure/cli-foo/target/cli-foo-0.1.0-SNAPSHOT-
standalone.jar
Creating standalone executable: /Users/M/code/clojure/cli-foo/target/
integralist
Copying binary to /usr/local/bin
```

If you now execute `integralist -vvv abc` you should see the expected output displayed on your screen. Great! We've created an executable that we can now run from anywhere on our system. But be aware that this executable is only going to work for the OS from where you built it. In order for the executable to work on another OS, you would need to build it from that OS architecture.

> ■ **Note** One option would be to utilize Docker,[5] which allows you to run different operating systems from your own computer. You could then build a docker image from the specific OS you want your application to work with and set up the environment to have Leiningen and the `lein-bin` plugin and compile the executable from within the Docker container by mounting your code base into the Docker container at runtime. Docker is outside the scope of this book, so we won't discuss this option further.

Flags Revisited

OK, let's now review the flags that we defined to make sure we understand their configuration. Let's start with the -p flag.

If I were to execute the `integralist` command with no flags defined, then I would see from the output that the -p (--port) flag was given the default value of 80. Looking back at Listing 13-2, we can see that's because we configured the :default attribute with that value. This means if I execute `integralist -p 123`, we expect to see 123 assigned to that flag in the command's output (which we do). This demonstrates how we can make certain flags optional by defining a default value.

If I were to execute `integralist -p abc`, then the output from the command would be an error (see Listing 13-11). We can see from the error that it was expecting a number, but the input was abc. If we look back at Listing 13-2, we can see this is because we configured the -p flag with a :parse-fn attribute, which allows us to convert the input into another format value (in this case, we assigned an anonymous function to :parse-fn that tries to convert the input into an integer).

Listing 13-11. Error from -p Flag Assigned an Incorrect Type

```
[Error while parsing option "-p abc": java.lang.NumberFormatException: For
input string: "abc"]
```

Similar to the :parse-fn attribute is the :validate attribute, which allows us to verify that the input's value is what we expect/need it to be. In this case, we want to ensure the number is within a specific range. If I passed 65535 as the value, then everything would work fine. But if I passed 99999, then we'd see an error (Listing 13-12).

Listing 13-12. Error from -p Flag Assigned an Incorrect Value

```
[Failed to validate "-p 99999": Must be a number between 0 and 65536]
```

If we now look at the -v flag, we can see it has two attributes we've not explained yet, :id and :assoc-fn. The :id attribute is required only if you've not defined a long flag. This is because the cli tools have a convention whereby they use the name of the long flag as a key inside the :options map data structure. With the -v flag, we've not provided a long flag (hence the use of the nil value).

---

[5]https://www.docker.com/

In some command-line tools, you'll see a convention whereby a defined flag can actually be dynamic. For example, if your tool allowed the showing of debug information, you might want the user to be able to configure how much debug info they see based on a "level." This is what we're trying to represent with the verbosity flag (-v) in our tool. So, if you execute `integralist -v`, you'll see the verbosity value is set to 1, but if you changed the flag to -vv, it would be set to 2, and again if you changed the flag to -vvv, it would be set to 3 (and so on).

This is what `:assoc-fn` is used for. It accepts the entire `:options` map data structure along with the flag `:id` and its current value (in our case, there was a `:default` value of 0 set). With that information, we can see in Listing 13-2 that we simply increment the flag's value inside the `:options` map.

■ **Note** We won't review the -x or -h flags, as they effectively just use the `:id` and `:default` attributes we've already seen.

Summary

In this chapter, we've taken a brief tour of some of the most important features from Clojure's `tools.cli`. We've learned how to create the shell for a command-line application that defines a set of flags with a varied set of conditions and behavioral expectations. This includes dynamic flags such as -v for defining debug verbosity levels and the -p flag, which requires the value be something that can be coerced into an integer and also be within a specific numerical range. There are other features available within `tools.cli`, and I recommend you go exploring to see how you might utilize them.

The other item covered was how to run the cli via Leiningen—a Jar or via a binary. The last two options mean you can take the single packaged file (or binary) and easily distribute your application to any system that has Java available.

APPENDIX A

Conventions

Every programming language has its own conventions for ensuring a collective understanding and consistency with the design of code written in that language. Some conventions are also able to transition pretty consistently across different programming languages due to the fact that there are groupings of languages (such as C) where the syntax is similar, and so the conventions make sense when applied across multiple languages.

For example, if you've ever written a for loop (of any variety), then chances are you'll know of the variable identifiers i, j, and k being used as characters for each nested loop level (see Listing A-1, which utilizes the JavaScript language syntax to demonstrate a for loop).

Listing A-1. Example of i, j, and k Variables in a for Loop

```
for (i = 0; i < condition; i++) {
    for (j = 0; j < condition; j++) {
        for (k = 0; k < condition; k++) {
            // code
        }
    }
}
```

■ **Note** i, j, and k are typically used for a few reasons (depending on who you talk to): i and j have been used in mathematics for a very long time, and so the transition of math to programming persisted. On a practical level, i is sometimes interpreted to stand for *integer*, and so when needing a nested level, it made sense to start moving up the alphabet to j, then k.

Clojure has similar naming conventions.

© Mark McDonnell 2017
M. McDonnell, *Quick Clojure*, DOI 10.1007/978-1-4842-2952-1

Functions

- f, g, h: function input (notice similarity with i, j, k, where now f represents *function*)

- n: integer input (usually a size)

- i: integer index

- x, y: numbers

- s: string input

- xs: considered a plural, or sequence, of x

- coll: a collection (or sequence)

- pred: a predicate closure

- & more: variadic input

- *var*: dynamic variables should be wrapped in asterisks (also referred to as "ear muffs")

Macros

- expr: an expression

- body: a macro body

- binding: a macro binding vector

APPENDIX B

∎ ∎ ∎

Writing Clojure with Vim

There are many text/code editors available on the market, each with its pros and cons and justifications as to why you should use it. Here is a short list that I managed to put together of editors that had some form of Clojure support available within them (or via plugins):

- Atom: Proto REPL

- Emacs: CIDER

- Vim: Fireplace

- IntelliJ (Java IDE): Cursive

- Light Table: Built-in Interactive Clojure IDE

As you can probably tell by the title of this appendix, I'm a Vim user. Now, I'm not going to sell you on the virtues of why I feel Vim is the best editor to use, as I've already done that by writing a book on the topic called *Pro Vim*[1] (published by Apress). Also, Vim does have quite a steep learning curve, so it's not ideal for everyone.

That being said, if you're interested in using Vim for Clojure and/or you're already a Vim user, then stick with me while I cover the different plugins and configuration settings you'll need in order to get working efficiently with Clojure in Vim.

To start with, we need the following plugins installed:

- vim-fireplace[2]

- vim-sexp-mappings-for-regular-people[3]

- rainbow_parentheses.vim[4]

Now I'm going to run through these plugins in *reverse* order, because the preceding list is actually in *priority* order (i.e., the Fireplace plugin is essential, but the next two plugins, although very useful, strictly speaking aren't "essential" in order to have something working).

---

[1]http://www.apress.com/gb/book/9781484202517
[2]https://github.com/tpope/vim-fireplace/
[3]https://github.com/tpope/vim-sexp-mappings-for-regular-people/
[4]https://github.com/kien/rainbow_parentheses.vim

But also, the complexity of each plugin matches its priority and importance. So, for example, the lowest-priority plugin, Rainbow Parentheses, is also the easiest to describe.

Rainbow Parentheses

This plugin is very easy to work with. It takes all your boring parentheses and makes them color coded (that's it). The point is to make it easier to decipher the start and end of a particular Clojure form.

You might wonder: Why bother? But trust me, even with a Clojure file format theme, your eyes will still struggle to pick out specific forms in your code (especially because as your code becomes more complex you'll find there are lots of nested parentheses to deal with), and so having them rainbow colored is a real blessing.

Sexp Mappings for Regular People

In a Lisp-based language, you have what are referred to as S-expressions.[5] In layman's terms, these are simply part of a notation format, and you see them in Lisp-based languages as parentheses wrapped around expressions (this comes back to the "code as data" mantra we discussed at the beginning of the book, where code represents the same underlying data structure).

So, this plugin allows you to manipulate your Clojure code (e.g., the Clojure "forms"). But it's important to not get this plugin confused with another Vim plugin called Sexp,[6] which is a valid plugin for manipulating S-expressions. But the plugin we're interested in here is actually an extension of Sexp, just with more idiomatic key bindings for terminal-based Vim users.

There are two primary functions of this plugin:

1. Automatic Parentheses Matching

2. List Manipulation

The first item is fairly straightforward: if you type an opening parenthesis (, then Vim will automatically insert a closing parenthesis) after it and will then place your cursor in-between the parentheses. This is great because it saves you from forgetting to add either an opening or closing parenthesis yourself, which could accidentally cause your program to trigger an error (this can be quite an annoying bug to have to fix, as it can be difficult to identify when dealing with heavily nested forms).

The second item, list manipulation, is the crux of this plugin. It provides the following key bindings:

- <f and >f: move "form" left or right

- <e and >e: move "element" left or right

---

[5] https://en.wikipedia.org/wiki/S-expression
[6] https://github.com/guns/vim-sexp

- `<(` and `>(`: move "opening parenthesis" left or right
- `<)` and `>)`: move "closing parenthesis" left or right
- `<I` and `>I`: move "insertion" left or right

Let's do some quick demonstrations to highlight how these key bindings work. We'll assume we're dealing with the following code (see Listing B-1), and after each manipulation we'll compare back to Listing B-1 to see how things have changed.

Listing B-1. A Simple Function That Handles a Calculation

```
(def myfn [f g h]
  (* h (+ f g)))
```

Form Manipulation

The key bindings `<f` and `>f` affect the innermost form your cursor currently resides within. So, if your cursor is inside (or on top of) the form `(+ f g)` and you execute `<f`, then you'll find that the form moves to the left (see Listing B-2 for the new layout).

Listing B-2. Result from Form Manipulation

```
(def myfn [f g h]
  (* (+ f g) h))
```

Element Manipulation

Similar to form manipulation, if your cursor is on top of the h symbol (i.e., "element") and you execute `>e` on the original example code, then you'll find that it moves the element to the right (see Listing B-3 for the new layout).

Listing B-3. Result from Element Manipulation

```
(def myfn [f g h]
  (* (+ f g) h))
```

■ **Note**   You'll see that Listing B-3 reached the same output as Listing B-2, but it was achieved by two different mechanisms.

Parenthesis Manipulation

If your cursor is on top of (or inside of) the `(` character from `(+ f g)`, and you execute `2<(` on the original example code, then you'll find that it moves the parenthesis two places to the left (see Listing B-4 for the new layout). In this example, I've used a Vim count of 2 with `<(`, so it is run twice.

Listing B-4. Result from Parenthesis Manipulation

```
(def myfn [f g h]
  ((* h + f g)))
```

■ **Note**   This code would now cause an error when run, but I've done this to demonstrate the functionality (because of the automatic parenthesis-insertion feature, I very rarely need to manipulate an individual parenthesis).

Insertion Manipulation

If your cursor is on top of (or inside of) a form, then executing <I will move your cursor to the start of the form and automatically enter Vim's INSERT mode. As an example, place your cursor inside (+ f g) and execute <I; you should see that the cursor is placed before the +, ready for you to start typing.

Similarly, if you were to place your cursor inside the (* h ...), making sure it's outside of the (+ f g) form (which is nested inside), and then execute >I; you would see that the cursor is placed just before the form's closing parenthesis. This feature is useful for quickly getting to the start and end of long and complex forms.

Fireplace

The Fireplace plugin is the main event. With this plugin, you can connect Vim to a networked REPL (Leiningen, in our case, but there are others you can use if you want to) and dynamically evaluate your Clojure code right from within Vim. This would result in your getting instant feedback on the code you've written and how it will actually behave. This is an incredibly powerful and enlightening development experience.

■ **Note**   Many people are confused by the name of this plugin: Why is it called Fireplace? It's all in the name: fi-REPL-ace (notice REPL in the middle).

Steps Required

The principal steps we need to take are as follows:

1. Start our REPL.

2. Open a Clojure file in Vim.

3. Run the :Connect Fireplace command.

4. Enter our REPL details into the Vim prompt.

After these steps have been completed, we can then start using Fireplace-specific key bindings to evaluate our Clojure code.

Preferred Workflow?

Your workflow may differ from mine (most Vim users have their own way of doing things). For me, I use NeoVim,[7] and so I have the ability to create a split window that contains an actual terminal instance (e.g., using its :terminal command). So, for me, I'll have a horizontal split set of windows. In the top window would be my Clojure code, and in the bottom window would be my terminal (which is where I start up my REPL).

You might not use NeoVim, but that doesn't matter. If you're a tmux[8] user, then you can have a horizontal split pane that does effectively the same thing. If you don't use a terminal multiplexer like tmux or screen,[9] then you can simply start up two shell/terminal instances; you'll have to jump back and forth between them for the initial set-up steps I'm about to detail.

Connecting to the REPL

OK, so let's begin by starting up our REPL: lein repl

Before we can connect to a REPL from Vim using the Fireplace plugin, we need to have a Clojure file open; this is because Fireplace only loads up its functionality if it finds a Clojure-formatted file (if you try to run any of its commands from a different file type, then Vim will state it doesn't recognize the command).

In Vim you have the option of either opening a Clojure file or simply opening an empty buffer and setting the format of the buffer to be a Clojure file; for example, setf clojure. It doesn't matter which one you choose. Typically, if I want to just mess around with some Clojure code, then I'll start up Vim with an empty buffer and use setf clojure (I'm sure some people would argue for using Leiningen's REPL directly, but I prefer working within Vim); otherwise, if I'm working on an actual project, I'll open up the Clojure file I want to edit.

Once we've done that, Vim will be able to use the :Connect command that Fireplace provides. With this command you can use tab completion to fill in most of the required values; type in the values directly like so :Connect <VALUE>; or press ENTER to have Vim automatically prompt you for answers. I usually just type in what we need :Connect nrepl://127.0.0.1:65103.

If you're wondering where I got the 127.0.0.1:65103 (which is <LOCAL_IP>:<PORT_NUMBER>) from, then look no further than the screen where you ran lein repl. You should see that the first line of output looks something like what's shown in Listing B-5, and once connected you will see a message similar to Listing B-6.

---

[7]http://neovim.io/
[8]https://tmux.github.io/
[9]https://www.gnu.org/software/screen/

Listing B-5. Abstract Output from lein repl Command

```
nREPL server started on port <PORT_NUMBER>
on host <LOCAL_IP> -
nrepl://<LOCAL_IP>:<PORT_NUMBER>
```

■ **Note**   You can just use localhost instead of 127.0.0.1

Listing B-6. Vim Output Once Connected to REPL

```
Connected to nrepl://<LOCAL_IP>:<PORT_NUMBER>
Scope connection to: <path/to/your/project>
```

To close this message, press ENTER.

■ **Note**   The syntax structure of the :Connect command is: <PROTOCOL>://<LOCAL_ IP>:<PORT_NUMBER> <PATH/TO/CODE>. But be aware that the path to your project code shouldn't have spaces. For example, ~/Some/Project is fine but ~/Some Other/Project would not work.

Fireplace Commands

There are quite a few Fireplace key bindings and commands, so I would strongly recommend you have a read of the Fireplace help documents (:help fireplace), as I won't attempt to cover all of them. Hell, some of them I've never used! But the ones I use the most I've included details for here (I urge you to try out the examples given so you get a feel for them).

- :Doc <symbol> (e.g., :Doc defn)
- :FindDoc <symbol> (e.g., :FindDoc de)
- :Source <symbol> (e.g., :Source defn)

■ **Note**   Executing the K key binding while the cursor is on top of a symbol is a shortcut for the :Doc command. If you need to exit the :FindDoc results screen you can either press Q or keep scrolling until you reach the bottom and then press ENTER. Also, executing the [d or]d key bindings while the cursor is on top of a symbol is a shortcut for the :Source command.

Fireplace Key Bindings

- cpp: evaluates innermost form

- cqp: displays prompt to enter custom expression

- cqq: displays prompt with current form prepopulated

- cqc: displays prompt within command-line window

- cmm: Expands a Clojure macro

In Listing B-7, we can see an example function called calc, which we will use as the basis for exploring the key bindings shown in the preceding list. For the purposes of the following sections, let's add that code into a new empty buffer with setf clojure (rather than run it from an actual project directory).

Listing B-7. Example Function to Verify Key Bindings Against

```
(defn calc [f g]
  (* (+ f g) (/ g f)))
```

cpp

Place your cursor on the first line of Listing B-7 (i.e., (defn calc [f g]) and execute the key binding cpp. You should see the result displayed at the bottom of your Vim instance: #'user/calc.

You'll notice the namespace is user because we're working in a buffer that's not been written to a file. If we were working from a real Clojure project, you might see something like: #'<path/to/your/project/namespace>/calc instead.

If you were to execute the cpp key binding while your cursor was placed on top of a function call (e.g., (calc 100 50)), then it would evaluate that call and return the actual result. But be aware that if (in this example) you hadn't already executed cpp on the calc function definition itself (i.e., the REPL hadn't evaluated the function definition), then you would have found that the REPL could not evaluate the call to the calc function as it wouldn't know where to locate it. This would result in an error (see Listing B-8).

Listing B-8. Error Evaluating Call to a Function That Wasn't Evaluated

```
CompilerException java.lang.RuntimeException:
Unable to resolve symbol: calc in this context, compiling:(4:1)
```

This type of error occurs when you forget to evaluate the function definition; e.g., you enter lots of code and then just try to call it without evaluating individual definitions first. Sometimes it can be easier to just re-evaluate the entire buffer at once, which you can do using :%Eval (that might be something you stick in a custom key binding just to make it quicker and easier to execute).

cqp

Executing the key binding cqp anywhere in the current buffer will result in Vim's displaying a command prompt for you to enter a new expression to be evaluated. As before, if you try to evaluate definitions found within your code, make sure the REPL knows about them by evaluating the definition you want to use, or by re-evaluating the entire buffer first.

cqq

The cqq key binding works by taking the form under the cursor in the current buffer and placing it into the Vim command prompt, where you can then modify the command before pressing ENTER to evaluate the expression.

■ **Note**   I've found that NeoVim, when using a :terminal pane, will not display the evaluation of the cqq key binding. The eval does happen (we know this by checking :Last, which shows the last Clojure evaluation within a preview window); it just isn't displayed. This is believed to be a bug.

---

cqc

The cqc key binding can be executed anywhere within your current buffer. It'll open the Vim command-line window, allowing you to search through previous evaluations and modify them before re-evaluating.

cmm

The cmm key binding is really useful for understanding how macros work underneath the abstraction (i.e., what the code looks like once the macro has been expanded). Consider the calc function we've been working with; if we execute cmm on the definition, then macro expansion will evaluate this to what's shown in Listing B-9.

Listing B-9. Defn Macro Expanded Using cmm Key Binding

```
(def calc (fn* ([f g] (* (+ f g) (/ g f)))))
```

In Listing B-9, we can see that the execution of cmm on the defn macro expands it so that we can see how, in reality, the calc definition is really just a def form. It also shows the underlying use of an anonymous function to achieve what defn was abstracting away for us.

Index

© Mark McDonnell 2017
M. McDonnell, *Quick Clojure*, DOI 10.1007/978-1-4842-2952-1

Get the eBook for only $5!

Why limit yourself?

With most of our titles available in both PDF and ePUB format, you can access your content wherever and however you wish—on your PC, phone, tablet, or reader.

Since you've purchased this print book, we are happy to offer you the eBook for just $5.

To learn more, go to http://www.apress.com/companion or contact support@apress.com.

Apress®

Printed in the United States
By Bookmasters